ARIZONA

KICKS ON ROUTE 66

W9-BXF-705

RIO NUEVO PUBLISHERS

Text by Roger Naylor
Photographs by Larry Lindahl

Rio Nuevo Publishers®
P.O. Box 5250, Tucson, Arizona 85703-0250
(520) 623-9558, www.rionuevo.com

Text copyright © 2011 by Roger Naylor.
Photos copyright © 2011 by Larry Lindahl.
Roger Naylor photo by Cody DeLong. Larry Lindahl
photo by Nina Rehfeld.

All rights reserved. No part of this book may be
reproduced, stored, introduced into a retrieval system,
or otherwise copied in any form without the prior
written permission of the publisher, except for brief
quotations in reviews or citations.

Design: Julie Sullivan Design, Flagstaff, AZ.

Printed in USA.

13   12

Library of Congress Cataloging-in-Publication Data
Naylor, Roger (Roger James), 1957-
Arizona kicks on Route 66 / text by Roger Naylor ;
photographs by Larry Lindahl.
    p. cm.
ISBN-13: 978-1-933855-76-9 (pbk. : alk. paper)
ISBN-10: 1-933855-76-2 (pbk. : alk. paper)
1. Arizona--Description and travel. 2. United States
Highway 66. 3. Arizona—History, Local. 4. Automobile
travel—Arizona. I. Lindahl, Larry, photographer. II.
Title.
F815.N39 2012
917.9104'54--dc23
                            2011045630

To my wife, Michele, because road trips—and life—are
best enjoyed with someone amazing in the passenger seat.
                            —R.N.

For my dad, George Lindahl (1923–2004).
                            —L.L.

CONTENTS

Background: Sierra Vista Motel in Flagstaff
Right, from top to bottom:
Peach Springs postcard
Dinosaurs of the Rainbow Rock Shop in Holbrook
Betty Boop of Goldie's Route 66 Diner in Williams
A 1964 Chevrolet Impala SS in Peach Springs

Introduction

Known as the "Main Street of America," Route 66 stretched from Chicago to Los Angeles. Along the way it passed through eight states. Eventually the advent of the interstate system—those hauntingly efficient, suffocating superslabs—shunted meandering Route 66 aside.

After its decertification in 1985, U.S. 66 officially ceased to exist. Unofficially, Route 66 vaulted from pop culture icon to near mythic status. Route 66 has become a symbol of freedom, of innocence, a symbol of the last good time America ever had.

While each of the eight states fiercely protects its portion of Route 66, the Arizona segment stands out. Arizona is where the Route 66 preservation movement began, and where the road was first declared Historic Route 66. Over 200 miles of the original highway are still drivable in Arizona, including the longest unbroken stretch in existence. And it is a voyage set against a profoundly dazzling, soul-nudging landscape.

Route 66 Arizona delivers the frontier. The Wild West, the epic West, the West of legend envelops the old road. The scenery bites your heart in half.

Route 66 Arizona crosses stark badlands, cloud-swept plateaus, and a desert painted in scandalous hues. The road explores forests of tall pines and forests where trees have turned to stone. It brushes past volcanoes, craters, the ruins of ancient civilizations, and one of the Seven Natural Wonders of the World.

The wavy two-lane rolls across shimmering grasslands and weaves through rocky canyons before traversing a torturous mountain pass to finally meet the banks of the Colorado River. All along the way it is cradled by layers of Americana, both present-day and faded past. Amid the scenic splendor, the highway John Steinbeck referred to as the "Mother Road" passes through small towns and the skeletons of towns.

Route 66 Arizona delivers the frontier. The Wild West, the epic West, the West of legend envelops the old road. The scenery bites your heart in half.

Above: Historic Route 66 sign from the Snow Cap in Seligman.

You can find almost anything along Route 66 in Arizona, from petrified logs to giant jackrabbits to bronzed hitchhikers to dinosaurs to teepees, but no camels. That's strange because camels played a role in the history of the highway.

In 1857 Lieutenant Edward Beale was commissioned to survey a wagon road from Fort Defiance, New Mexico, to the Colorado River. Beale traveled the 35th Parallel and brought camels as pack animals. While Beale felt the dromedaries performed well, they spooked less-worldly horses and mules. So the camels were turned loose to roam the Mohave Desert. Their descendants were still being sighted after Route 66 debuted in 1926. Imagine weary drivers looking for a place to camp as twilight settled on the twisted shapes of Joshua trees. Coyote howls already have them on edge, when suddenly out of the shadows looms a great humped brute, a shaggy beast that spits on their windshield as they speed past. It's a miracle Arizona ever got tourists to return.

Route 66 changed the landscape of communities that had been geared to satisfying the needs of railroad passengers. Towns spread away from the tracks as gas stations, cafes, and tourist camps opened. "With the opening of the highway," says Sean Evans, archivist at Northern Arizona University, "travelers were able to experience all sorts of things that the railroad would not have permitted or entertained. Food, languages, arts and crafts, all sorts of different cultural ideas and beliefs intersected in the cafes, tourist traps, trading posts, and motels along the way."

During the '30s, massive dust storms pushed thousands of "Okies" onto Route 66, seeking work in the promised lands of California. Angel Delgadillo of Seligman, who spearheaded the Route 66 preservation movement, remembers those days. "Those poor Okies would

Clockwise, from top: Route 66 climbs the mountains between Cool Springs and Sitgreaves Pass in a twisted spiral of brake-searing curves. Early travelers get their kicks on Route 66. Before automobiles, America traveled by train.

MOHAVE MUSEUM OF HISTORY & ARTS

OLD TRAILS MUSEUM

drive through town in rattletrap vehicles that didn't look like they had many more miles in them," says Delgadillo. "They'd be loaded down with tools and spare tires and mattresses and washtubs and chickens. They looked so tired, but the road kept going west and so did they."

World War II made Route 66 a thoroughfare to move troops and equipment to installations such as the Navajo Army Depot in Bellemont and the Kingman Army Airfield, where over 36,000 bomber gunners trained. War industry jobs in California brought a fresh wave of migrating workers.

In the post-war boom, Americans went road tripping and Route 66 hit the full gaudy flower of its heyday. Many followed the advice of Bobby Troupe's hit song recorded in 1946 and got their kicks on Route 66. Yet even during the golden age of tourism, the seeds of its demise were being sown. In 1957 President Eisenhower instituted the National Interstate Highway System. On October 13, 1984, Interstate 40 was officially opened and the town of Williams had the distinction of being the last town bypassed by the freeway. Route 66 was quietly decertified.

Angel Delgadillo remembers, "one day there was so much traffic in Seligman, it might take 15 minutes to cross the street. The next day you could lie down in the middle of the road and not worry about getting run

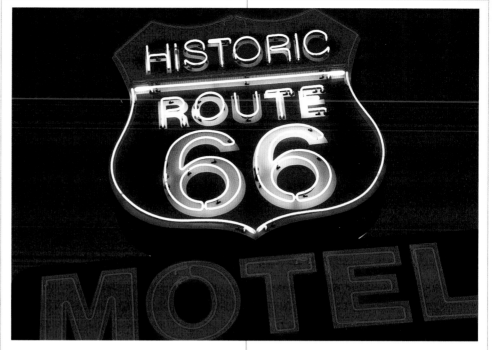

over. It's like the world just forgot we existed." Several communities simply vanished, but Angel was determined not to let that happen to Seligman. In 1987, Angel, along with other local business owners, formed the Historic Route 66 Association of Arizona. They lobbied the state to designate Route 66 a historic highway. By the very next year, the state had agreed and began posting appropriate signage. It was the first historic designation for the road that no longer existed.

Soon organizations sprang up in other states and a wave of Route 66 nostalgia was underway. For his tireless efforts to preserve and promote the highway, Angel Delgadillo is known as the Mayor of Route 66, and was honored as an Arizona Culturekeeper.

"I am surprisingly optimistic about where Route 66 is and where it might go," says Sean Evans. "I'm happy to see cities and towns re-embracing the road. They see that 66 brings tourists and that means jobs and opportunities. Every town that re-embraces Route 66 is also reexamining their past at a much broader level. Any time we think about our past, I believe good things happen."

Today, grand adventures mingled with intimate moments unfold along Route 66 Arizona, while conjuring images of simpler times. Places still exist where diners are run by sassy waitresses who call everybody "Hon," where motel rooms are shaped like teepees and neon signs paint the night softly.

We'll travel Route 66 across Arizona, moving east to west because that is the natural rhythm of things. It's a beautiful, bewitching drive with amazing side trips. Grand Canyon anyone? Sedona?

Plus, there's pie. We'll stop often for pie. Roll the window down and buckle up.

Above: The seductive neon of the Historic Route 66 Motel in Seligman entices visitors to stop for the night. *Left:* The distinctive 1955 Ford Crown Victoria is usually parked in front of Twisters 50's Soda Fountain in Williams.

ROUTE 66 ARIZONA FACTS

- Arizona contains the longest unbroken stretch of Route 66 still in existence, 158 miles from west of Ash Fork to the California border.

- Arizona is the birthplace of Historic Route 66. Through the work of a handful of Seligman residents, Arizona became the first state to dedicate a stretch of U.S. 66 as Historic Route 66, thus beginning the preservation efforts that encompassed the entire road.

- The only national park that Route 66 passes through is Petrified Forest National Park in Arizona.

- In 2009, Historic Route 66 in Arizona was designated an All-American Road under the Federal Highways National Scenic Byways Program. Only 37 roads in the nation have the distinction of being All-American Roads, roads that are destinations unto themselves. It is the only portion of Route 66 to receive such an honor.

- The longest curve, the steepest grade, and the highest point on Route 66 are in Arizona.

- The Arizona leg of Route 66 follows the wagon trail laid out by Lieutenant Edward Beale and his exotic caravan of soldiers and camels in 1857.

- The last Route 66 town to be bypassed by the interstate was Williams, Arizona.

- Arizona is home to the largest collection of national parks, national monuments, and national recreation areas within an hour's drive of Route 66. They include the Grand Canyon, Petrified Forest, Canyon de Chelly, Wupatki, Sunset Crater, Walnut Canyon, Montezuma Castle, Montezuma Well, Tuzigoot, and Lake Mead.

A weathered motel sign in the ghost town of Yucca sits on a 1952 Route 66 alignment near Kingman. *Opposite:* The unmistakable thrust of Boundary Cone rises west of Oatman.

CHAPTER 1

Navajoland

TRADING POST ROW

Above: Medallions adorn a tattered sign outside Route 66 Diner in Sanders. *Right:* A herd of fiberglass animals stand watch over the Chief Yellowhorse Trading Post from the ground and the cliffs above. *Opposite:* Horses graze in the shadow of soaring sandstone cliffs in Lupton.

Arizona puts out an emphatic welcome mat. Soon as you cross the state line from New Mexico, big sandstone cliffs bully their way forward, push right up to the edge of the highway. Pull off I-40 at Exit 359 and man, they just loom. Sheer walls of sandstone soar overhead, a brutish thrust of eroded rock that makes you want to stumble from the car gawking in wonder. It won't be the last time on this journey.

Lupton

A cluster of shops in shades of yellow and red are strung along the base of the cliffs. Most of these form the Chief Yellowhorse Trading Post. Fiberglass animals perch on a ledge above the buildings. Billboards frame the rickety row of structures. Chief Juan Yellowhorse, a former Navy airman, bought the property in 1960 and put his distinctive stamp on it, even keeping corralled bison on display for a few years. The trading post continues to be operated by members of his family.

Besides the Yellowhorse complex, Lupton contains the Painted Cliffs Welcome Center, a shiny outpost of the Arizona Office of Tourism. There's a general store and the Tomahawk Indian Store, housed in "the largest teepee in the Southwest."

Since this is the first of many encountered, it should be noted that teepees were used by Plains Indians, not Navajos. Neither did Navajos wear feathered headdresses, like those seen in shops and on signs. But flavor outweighs facts. It's about giving the customers what they want. For generations, Route 66 in Arizona afforded easterners their first encounter with Native Americans. Thanks to Hollywood, travelers held a certain perception of Indians and the

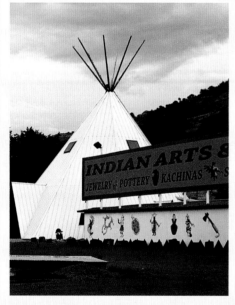

Navajos were business-savvy enough to comply.

Once finished with souvenir shopping, cross under the interstate and turn west on the southern frontage road, an old Route 66 alignment. Look for Elephant Rock among the burly cliffs to the south. The formation outlines a pachyderm from the rear yet glancing over his right shoulder back in your direction, as if your pockets were stuffed with peanuts. More importantly, keep an eye peeled for my horses.

It's a Route 66 moment. I brake for horses. They stand in the road grazing on tall grass at the edge of the pavement.

I'm stopped on an old alignment of Mother Road on the Navajo Reservation just inside the New Mexico border because this is still open range country. This is still the West. I could ease forward and nose the horses out of the road, but why would I do that? If making "good time" were a priority I would be careening down the nearby interstate, cocooned and detached.

Instead, I sit idling. I watch the overripe late-day sun melt down sandstone cliffs like warm honey.

I ogle clouds wafting by like soft, fat planets. I lean out the window and listen for several minutes in the cradling stillness, to horses chomping sweet grass.

It's a Route 66 Arizona moment.

Left: The Tomahawk Indian Store claims the "Largest Teepee in the Southwest."
Below: Visitors from the east get their first introduction to Navajos at the Chief Yellowhorse Trading Post that straddles the Arizona–New Mexico border.

Navajo Nation

The eastern portion of Route 66 Arizona passes through the Navajo Nation, the largest Native American reservation in the country. Navajoland sprawls across 27,000 square miles of northeastern Arizona into Utah and New Mexico. It is characterized by high plateaus, arid deserts, and alpine forests. Things to keep in mind while on the reservation:

The Navajo Nation recognizes Daylight Saving Time even though the state of Arizona does not.

Cameras are not always welcome. Ask permission before photographing a Navajo, and a gratuity is appreciated.

After five miles, turn north and jump on I-40 (Exit 354), or continue along the frontage road for three more miles, which is probably no longer related to Route 66. And purists beware: This is not a turn-by-turn book. If you're looking to track down every Route 66 fragment, every orphaned patch of pavement, every weed-choked tire rut from an ancient alignment, other resources can provide that sort of gritty minutiae. I'll delve lightly into the amazing history of the highway but will focus more on the journey—the romance and joy, the mystery and grace.

Houck

Two more trading posts are found at Allentown Road (Exit 351). Chee's Indian Store started as a Navajo rug stand in 1948. The building went up in '70 and the same family still runs the place. Also on premises a hogan has been constructed, the traditional Navajo dwelling. Hogans have six or eight sides and are generally built with logs, brush, and mud. The doorway always faces east towards the rising sun.

Next-door to Chee's, Indian City is a newer pueblo-style building with a large teepee guarding the entrance. While locally handcrafted items can be found in all these roadside trading posts, most of the merchandise tends towards pre-packaged souvenir items.

Take the northern frontage road three miles to a testament of Route 66 weirdness. At Exit 348, bracketed by clusterbombs of gaudy billboards, stands Fort Courage Trading Post. It's a store fronted by the ramshackle facade of a western fort and based on the short-lived television sit-com, *F Troop*.

If you weren't a small boy in the mid-60s you probably don't remember F Troop. It aired from '65-67 and was sort of a *Gilligan's Island* set on the frontier. A collection of army misfits were stationed at Fort Courage. The main character was Sgt. O'Rourke, who, unbeknownst to his bumbling CO, secretly ran a string of moneymaking

Fort Courage was built in the 1960s to cash in on the popular TV show, *F Troop*. While *F-Troop* aired only from 1965–67, it is still fondly remembered by former fans. At least one anyway.

F TROOP MOMENT

PHOTOFEST

Corporal Agarn: I still say I've been seeing an Indian looking through that window.

Sergeant O'Rourke: And why would an Indian be looking through that window?

Corporal Agarn: How do I know? Maybe he's a peeping tomahawk.

Top: A billboard for Fort Courage may be ready for an update. Does anyone still use film? *Opposite:* The Route 66 Diner in Sanders is known for juicy burgers, thick shakes, and curious building additions.

ventures called O'Rourke Enterprises. His business partners were the local Indian tribe, the cowardly Hekawi. And if eight-year-old me is any kind of judge, *F Troop* was pure comedy gold.

That was the wobbly little star the builders of Fort Courage hitched their wagon to, and it paid off. Decades later it still does a comfortable business among interstate drones with full bladders, Route 66 travelers, and former eight-year-olds.

Fort Courage occupies a sweet section of Route 66. Turn west out of the parking lot. The pavement soon fades, but the dirt segment can be navigated in a carefully driven sedan. The ruins of the old Querino Trading Post perch on the hillside above a rugged canyon. The picturesque Querino Canyon Bridge, built in 1929, spans the high-walled gorge.

Stop and get out of your vehicle, if not for a photo, for a memory. All the elements—the scenery, the dusty hardpack, the narrow concrete and steel truss bridge—combine to create a true time capsule moment of early Route 66 travel.

Soon the pavement resumes and you pull into Indian Ruins Trading Post. A soda fountain and snack bar inside Indian Ruins add an extra element of refreshment possibilities. If you're fortunate you might find the octogenarian owner manning the store. Armand Ortega has owned trading posts along Route 66, in New York City, and around the world. To sip a root beer float and listen to the gracious gentleman spin tales is an adventure all by itself.

After 18 miles of two-lane, most on old Route 66, it's time to jump on I-40 (Exit 341), at least for a bit. A patchwork of Route 66 segments cradles the interstate as it flashes across the high desert. So there are plenty of stops along the way.

fun fact

There's a genuine Valentine Diner (oddly mated to a trailer) in Sanders. The Route 66 Diner is off Exit 339.

ARIZONA HISTORICAL SOCIETY, FLAGSTAFF

Top: Lorenzo Hubbell with a Navajo weaver and an oversized Navajo rug, ca. 1940.
Above: Ruby Hubbard demonstrates the patient art of rug weaving at the Hubbell Trading Post Visitor Center.
Opposite: Colorful hand-woven rugs are stacked in piles at historic Hubbell Trading Post.

SIDE TRIP

Hubbell Trading Post

With their souvenir and snack-intensive inventories, the trading posts scattered along Route 66 are obviously geared towards touristas. Yet a quick side trip from the Mother Road leads to the genuine article. Hubbell Trading Post, founded in 1876, is the oldest continuously operating trading post on the Navajo Reservation.

Named for Lorenzo Hubbell, this National Historic Site is part museum and part art gallery, but most importantly, it's still a fully functioning trading post, virtually unchanged in the past century-plus. Scuffed wooden floors creak at every step. The bullpen (store) is crowded with goods and spicy with old aromas. Foodstuffs and supplies line the shelves. Counters are stacked with bolts of cloth and skeins of wool. Frying pans, horse collars, and kerosene lanterns hang from the ceiling. Off the bullpen, a trader sits in the jewelry room, which also contains carvings, paintings, and clay work. In a third room, gorgeous handwoven rugs are stacked in casual piles.

"We still operate as we always have," trader Steve Pickle said. "We trade for cash or barter for things in the store."

Local artists bring handcrafted items to sell and people shop for groceries and supplies, just like the old days when trading posts were community centers and a bridge between Anglo and Navajo cultures. Hubbell was respected for his honest dealings, friendship, and wise counsel.

Rug weaving demonstrations take place in the visitor center, a great way to see the patient skill the process requires. Ranger-guided tours through the carefully preserved Hubbell home are offered and visitors are free to roam the shady grounds.

CHAPTER 2

Petrified Forest & Painted Desert

TREES OF STONE, LIGHT OF GLASS

PAINTED DESERT INN
PETRIFIED FOREST
NATIONAL MONUMENT
A R I Z O N A

MIKE WARD

Opposite: Toppled stone trees along the Blue Mesa Trail catch the glitter of sunset in Petrified Forest National Park.
Above: Painted Desert Inn was built in 1924 and later remodeled by Mary Colter.
Right: Cold Drinks are advertised on the Painted Desert Trading Post.

As you enter the park (Exit 311), the road loops onto a volcanic escarpment overlooking the softly gnawed badlands of the Painted Desert. Rolling plains break apart against low-shouldered hills. Crumbling siltstone banded with seams of color shimmer and change with the light. Until confronted with it, we forget how hauntingly beautiful barren can be. I wonder what it must have been like for vacationing Midwesterners seeing this dazzling desolation for the first time; like they had made a wrong turn somewhere and driven to the moon.

The Painted Desert portion of the park lies north of the interstate with most of the Petrified Forest occupying the southern section. A 28-mile scenic drive connects the two segments, with viewpoints, historic sites, and hiking trails along the way.

From a high perch, Painted Desert Inn commands sweeping views across the pastel-hued wilderness. Originally built in 1924, it operated as an inn until it was taken over by the park service. The Fred Harvey Company assumed control in '48 and brought in their ace architect, Mary Colter, for a remodel. (We'll learn more about Harvey and Colter in Winslow.)

Colter hired Hopi artist Fred Kabotie to paint vivid murals in two rooms. One of those designs, the Sun God, became the symbol for the Harvey Company. The inn closed with the coming of I-40 and sat empty for almost 30 years. Now listed as a National Historic Landmark, the building has been restored as a striking museum.

The last roadside pull-out before crossing over the interstate into the Petrified Forest commemorates Route 66. The rusted hull of a '30s roadster marks the spot and a string of weathered telephone poles traces the old alignment, a silent reminder of what once existed, like the chalk outline at a murder scene.

I walk out into the desert towards the poles and stand in the sand and the sage. The interstate traffic rumbles in the distance like muffled surf. I find a small stone marker and kick at crumbs of old asphalt. Squinting into the sun haze I see a tire track, as faint and haunting as an ex-lover's scent. But it's only a mirage. The desert is reclaiming the roadbed.

Continue south on the park's scenic drive across the Puerco River. Hard to imagine while gazing across this wind-scoured lunar landscape, but once a lush tropical jungle thrived here. During the Triassic Period this was a crazy petri dish of tropical plants and alligator-like creatures and dinosaurs. Massive trees toppled into swamps and streams and were buried beneath volcanic ash and slowly the woody tissue was replaced by dissolved silica. The process is a bit more complicated, but who do I look like, Mr. Science?

Petrified Forest National Park preserves one of the world's largest repositories of dinosaur bones, in addition to their more famous fossilized trees—which explains the brigade of fiberglass dinos loitering in front of shops across the region. Maybe you thought it was merely a kitschy gimmick, but it's actually an effort to educate. Also, dinosaurs are cool.

Left: Blending with the sparse landscape, Painted Desert Inn now operates as a museum. *Below:* A rusted car serves as monument to Route 66 in Petrified Forest National Park. The telephone poles trace the original alignment. *Opposite:* Puerco Pueblo was once a hundred-room village occupied by ancestral Puebloan people between A.D. 1250 and 1400.

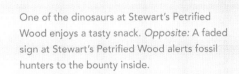

One of the dinosaurs at Stewart's Petrified Wood enjoys a tasty snack. *Opposite*: A faded sign at Stewart's Petrified Wood alerts fossil hunters to the bounty inside.

There are several historic sites, including the Puerco Pueblo and Agate House, the remains of ancient pueblos. Short hiking trails lead you into areas rich with petrified wood, where a shattered kaleidoscope of colorful stone fragments lie scattered about. In this day and age this shouldn't even need to be said, but please leave everything as you find it. The park service estimates a ton of petrified wood is stolen every MONTH. So stop it. Rock shops inside and outside the park will gladly sell all the petrified wood souvenirs you'll ever need.

Adamana Road

Drive a few miles west of Petrified Forest on I-40 and you find yourself surrounded by dinosaurs. Depart the freeway at Adamana Road (Exit 303), better known as Dinosaur Alley. (I actually just made that up but I'm hoping it catches on.)

Stewart's Petrified Wood, an old-school outpost, sits amid crumbling hills on the north side of the interstate. A ragtag herd of homemade dinosaurs fan out across the property and glare at you from high ground. At first glance they appear lumpy and cartoonish, but don't be fooled. They are fierce predators. Look closer and you'll notice many are chomping on human body parts.

Stewart's houses a collection of petrified wood, rocks, and gems in dusty bins. They also sell ostrich feed, which proves handy since several of the gangly birds are penned outside. Beware: the birds tend to be assertive when coming for food. One suspects that they wouldn't mind chomping on human body parts as well.

South of the interstate, Painted Desert Indian Center sports a newer, sleeker look. Their thunder lizards could be Jurassic Park stunt doubles. Some of the great roaring beasts grasp smaller animals in their powerful clutches. Yet even more frightening is the fact that the dinosaurs prowl among a village of teepees! Dinosaurs and wigwams. The potential carnage makes it impossible to resist.

Both Painted Desert Indian Center, with its impressive jewelry selection, and neighboring Stewart's are delicious throwbacks to the days when roadside attractions were garish, gaudy, and cluttered with enough eye candy to agitate the kids. It's all about making travelers do the thing they often hate … stop. Halt. End progress. Make them pull over and get out of the car. It's the ongoing battle to force travelers to cease forward motion and experience something firsthand. If you can bypass dinosaurs and wigwams, you're made of sterner stuff than I am.

If you're up for a bonus drive, a scenic alignment of Route 66 heads east from Painted Desert Indian Center for 3 to 4 miles before ending and affords views of an old timber bridge.

ARIZONA 66 ARIZONA MOMENT

I am alone in the badlands of the Painted Desert. I have a backcountry permit and have hiked out past Lithodendron Wash into the still evening air. My plan to pitch a tent was interrupted by a riotous sunset. The sky filled with mad, startling swirls of color, like Van Gogh emptying his pockets at the police station. The hills around me glowed electric.

I crouch in the gathering darkness trying to decide if it was the greatest sunset in history when suddenly, beyond the craggy grasp of the desert, the full moon rises. Big and loud and impossibly bright, it is a lurid moon, a transcendent moon, a moon from a forgotten age. No longer orbiting the earth but stalking it. Tides crash inside my canteen. Rustlers cower in their hideout. The moon howls while coyotes cover their ears. It peels the skin away from the night. I reach for my shades.

CHAPTER 3

Holbrook

WIGWAM DREAMS

olling off the interstate onto Route 66 in Holbrook (Exit 289) jolts you. This is the first town of substance and you expect it to bristle with history. Yet the eastern edge of Holbrook seems surprisingly new.

Four wide lanes are flanked on both sides by the usual off-ramp suspects: chain motels, fast food joints, and gas stations disrupted by a smattering of older businesses. Driving this

corporate gauntlet you wonder what happened to Holbrook of yesteryear, and then Old Double Six dips beneath an interstate overpass and there it is, starting with a vintage Dairy Queen crowned by a dollop of stylish neon. That's followed by a welcome mix of older motels, restaurants, saloons, rock shops, and lurking dinosaurs.

Your first stop should be the historic Navajo County Courthouse. Built in 1898, the graceful courthouse now functions as visitor center with a busy little museum. Exhibits represent all eras of Holbrook history. You can even explore the claustrophobia-inducing jail cells adorned with prisoner-scrawled art.

Opposite: A revitalized Holbrook celebrates its Route 66 heritage with icons such as the Wigwam Motel. *Below:* A vintage Dairy Queen is one of the little gems found along Route 66 in Holbrook.

While at the courthouse grab a guidebook for the historical self-guided tour of the town, including the scene of the infamous Blevins shootout. This was part of the Pleasant Valley War, the bloodiest feud in American history. Sheriff Commodore Perry Owens (yes, that was his given name) tried to serve a warrant on Andy Blevins. But at the Blevins house words were exchanged and weapons brandished. Sheriff Owens, who could have swaggered off the pages of a dime novel with his flowing waist-length hair and steely-eyed gun skill, triggered his Winchester. In less than a minute, Owens fired five times, killing three and wounding a fourth.

As a western buff, I love Holbrook and its rowdy past. In 1886, 26 men died by gunshot. At the time, the population was only 250. Tombstone is known as The Town Too Tough to Die. Holbrook was too busy carting away corpses to conjure up a spiffy slogan.

Every weekday evening in June and July, Native American dances take place on the lawn of the courthouse. Native Americans clad in colorful tribal garb perform traditional dances in the soft summer twilight. The rising and falling chants of the singers, the rhythmic drumbeats wash away the sounds of traffic and transport spectators to a

Top 10 Things I Learned from Western Movies

10. Anyone shot in the vicinity of a wooden railing will fall through the railing no matter the angle of the bullet.

9. Despite enthusiasm and good intentions, a posse never catches anyone.

8. Saguaro cactus, the red rocks of Sedona, and Monument Valley can be found in every Western state.

7. Even though they are referred to as six-shooters, pistols hold considerably more than six bullets.

6. Beverage-wise, you can't beat whiskey.

5. Besides grazing, cows enjoy nothing more than participating in a stampede.

4. Anyone who sets foot in the desert is assigned their own personal flock of buzzards to circle above them for the duration of their stay.

3. Most cowboys have lovely singing voices.

2. The sheriff is either the bravest or the most cowardly man in town.

1. Only someone with a death wish pulls iron on John Wayne.

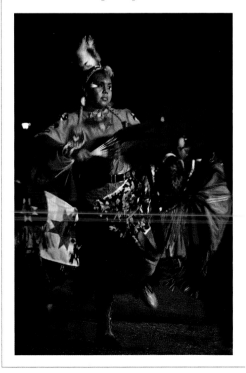

Clockwise from top: Built in 1898, the Navajo County Courthouse now houses a visitor center and museum. Ask about their resident ghost. • Visitors can tour the old jail in the basement of the courthouse that still displays prisoner-scrawled art. • Native American dances, swirls of movement and colors, take place on the courthouse lawn most summer evenings.

lonely mesa. It is a privilege to be part of something so powerful and ancient.

Just past the courthouse, Route 66 makes a 90-degree right turn. This is Hopi Drive and along this street you'll find Holbrook icons like Joe & Aggie's Café and the Wigwam Motel.

Joe & Aggie's Café

Our first pie stop isn't for pie at all, not in the traditional sense. But it will dance across your taste buds and isn't the fun of travel in embracing the new?

The eatery opened in 1943. Joe and Aggie Montano bought it two years later and it's been in the family ever since, with the third generation now dishing up a blend of Mexican and American cuisine. (The chile rellenos are light and heavenly!) The place also serves as a mini-museum with cases and shelves bowed beneath the weight of Route 66 memorabilia, including gifts and original artwork from John Lassiter, director of the Pixar movie Cars. Joe &

Aggie's Café is thanked in the credits as one of the inspirations for the cartoon's depiction of Route 66.

Their pie is actually a thermos-sized deep fried fruit burrito, like a naughty, naughty cousin of pie. A flour tortilla is stuffed with pie filling, deep fried, and dusted with powdered sugar and cinnamon. I try it à la mode because there are few problems in the world that can't be solved à la mode. The fruity pie richness bursts forth, masked only by the thin skin of tortilla.

Their pie is actually a thermos-sized deep fried fruit burrito, like a naughty, naughty cousin of pie.

Above: Route 66, the most definitive American highway, draws travelers from all over the globe. Francesco De Lisa is a member of the Harley Owners Group from Naples, Italy.

Below: Grab a window seat at Joe & Aggie's Café in the neon-bathed evenings and let Route 66 flow past.

Dinosaurs are a common sight on the streets of Holbrook due to the nearby fossil fields of Petrified Forest National Park. These great beasts, who oversee the Rainbow Rock Shop, were handmade by owner Adam Luna.

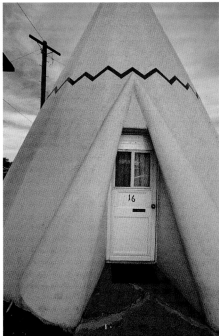

Chester Lewis opened the Wigwam Motel in 1950 and it became an instant Route 66 icon. *Opposite:* Vintage cars, like this 1959 Chevrolet Impala, parked in front of the units create a time-capsule quality at the Wigwam Motel.

Wigwam Motel

"Have you slept in a wigwam lately?" has been the marketing slogan for the Wigwam Motel for years, but it's also a finger jab to the psyche. It's a poignant reminder to evaluate your life and choices. How you answer the question says a lot about what kind of traveler, indeed what kind of person, you are. I never felt like a truly seasoned Arizona traveler until waking up in my own private teepee at Wigwam Motel.

Built by Chester Lewis, the Wigwam Motel opened in 1950 and became an instant Route 66 icon because frankly, a village of 32-foot-tall wigwams tends to catch the eye of travelers. Lewis was also an avid collector. A room filled with his artifacts can be found in the office.

"My father always dreamed of opening a museum," says Clifton Lewis, who operates the motel today with two siblings. "It never happened, but what he didn't realize, and I didn't at the time, was that the wigwams are his museum. This is his legacy."

The Lewis family has done a remarkable job preserving that legacy. Units are spotlessly clean, with angled walls forming a cozy teepee-like space, circular at the bottom and tapering upwards. Bathrooms are small but efficient. The mirror above the sink, attached to a slanted portion of wall, leans forward. I learned more about the top of my head than I cared to know. But the overall effect grabs you. You never forget you're sleeping in a wigwam.

Vintage cars parked in front of each unit complete the time capsule experience. I felt like a celebrity standing outside in the twilight as one motorist after another stopped to snap a photo. I slumbered, deep and well, content in the knowledge that I grew up to be the kind of person who sleeps in wigwams.

fun fact

Geronimo Trading Post (Exit 280) claims the World's Largest Petrified Tree, weighing 89,000 pounds.

Joseph City

At Exit 277, Route 66 swings through this sleepy burg. Big trees shade rambling country homes and form a quaint canopy at road's edge. With horses grazing in side yards, you could be motoring through bluegrass farmlands. The town forms a quiet contrast to the stark high-desert outposts typically found along this stretch of highway.

Originally known as Allen's Camp, Joseph City is the oldest Mormon community in Arizona. There are a few businesses mingled among the pastoral setting, but little acknowledgement of the Mother Road. Except at the western edge of town, there's an abandoned trading post still adorned with a mural of the 66 symbol, a map of Arizona, and curiously enough, Betty Boop.

At the end of town, turn left and cross over the interstate to the southern frontage road, where you'll turn right. Travel about five miles down this lumpy 66 alignment to a true icon of the road.

Jackrabbit Trading Post

Besides Bugs Bunny, Easter Bunny, and Energizer Bunny, the swoop-eared hare from the Jack Rabbit Trading Post logo may be the most famous carrot-muncher around.

This was originally a Santa Fe Railway building. Jack Taylor bought it in 1949, opened the Jack Rabbit Trading Post, and launched a brilliant marketing campaign. Eye-grabbing yellow billboards with the mysterious rabbit in profile and mileage number once stood in every state along Route 66. The closer you got, the mileage ticked down on the ensuing billboards and the rabbits grew larger, fostering a carload of suspense. "What's coming up? What could it be?" By the time travelers arrived in Joe City to find a big rabbit-adorned billboard trumpeting "Here It Is," not stopping was out of the question.

Taylor leased the store to Glenn Blansett in 1961, who bought it outright a few years later. It has stayed in the family, and is now operated by Blansett's granddaughter and her husband, Cindy and Tony Jaquez.

A giant saddled fiberglass rabbit outside provides a memorable photo op. The rabbit sits in a cement alcove wearing a hint of a smile. He's the Mona Lisa of overgrown jacks. He gazes across the distance and I like to think that at night, when his work shift ends, bounds off across the highway, across the railroad tracks into green fields beyond, where he terrorizes startled coyotes.

Above: The Geronimo Trading Post has been in business for over four decades. *Below:* Yuto Inoue of Japan captures a beloved Route 66 image, the Jackrabbit Trading Post billboard. *Opposite:* Great photo ops exist along Route 66 Arizona, and topping the list is the chance to climb in the saddle of a giant jackrabbit.

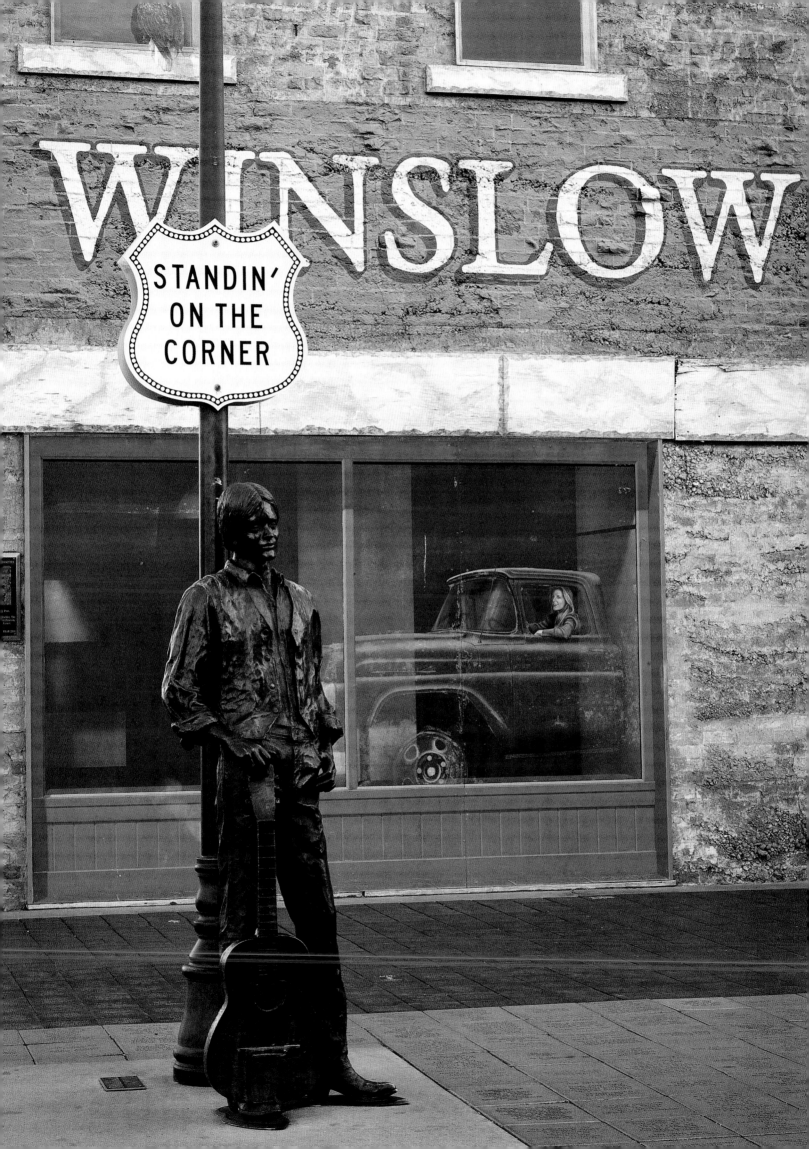

CHAPTER 4

Winslow to Winona

MADE FAMOUS IN SONG

Winslow took losing Route 66 right on the kisser. POW! Like a haymaker that buckled their knees, turned them glassy-eyed and wobbly before they dropped to the canvas. Looked like they were goners, but in the tradition of all cheesy, weepy fight movies, at the count of nine they staggered to their feet. Then POW! They got dropped again.

This went on for years, is still going on as a matter of fact. Until the 1960s, Winslow was the largest town in Northern Arizona. Two decades later it was a husk. That began to change in the mid-90s when a handful of people stepped up—which is the story of the Route 66 revival in a nutshell.

DRIVING ROUTE 66 THROUGH WINSLOW
Entering Winslow, depart the interstate at Exit 257. Go south across I-40, then turn right. The frontage road is old 66 and will take you into the historic district. Route 66 divided in 1951 through downtown, with westbound traffic following Third Street and eastbound, Second Street. Rejoin I-40 at Exit 252.

Opposite: It turns out Winslow is so much more than just a corner, although granted, it is a really cool corner.
Right: The Big Chief welcomes shoppers to Sweetland Furniture.

MIKE WARD

H-4158 DINING ROOM, LA POSADA, FRED HARVEY HOTEL, WINSLOW, ARIZONA

La Posada

It started with the saving of La Posada, the last great railroad hotel. Built in 1930 by the Fred Harvey Company, the opulent hotel was the finest on the Santa Fe line and became a magnet for the rich and famous. But rail travel declined and in '57 La Posada closed.

Soon afterwards, the Santa Fe Railway took one look at the airy, romantic hacienda-style building filled with artistic flourishes and awash in natural light and envisioned something even more magical…office space.

High wood-beamed ceilings were given the old acoustic tile makeover. Arched doorways were filled in to avoid confusion from those who might not recognize the graceful opening as a way to enter or exit a room. Stone floors were ripped up and replaced with stylish linoleum and intimidating natural light sealed out so as not to detract from the sallow glow of fluorescent bulbs.

In 1993 the railway announced plans to dispose of La Posada, apparently because they couldn't think of a way to turn it into a grain silo. That's when Allan Affeldt, his wife Tina Mion, and partner Dan Lutzick began negotiations and were finally able to purchase La Posada four years later. Massive restoration began immediately. They tore out the office facades and with the help of historic photos, recaptured the original look and artistic essence of Mary Colter's La Posada, complete with exquisite dining in the Turquoise Room.

Above: The dining room at La Posada, now the Turquoise Room, with windows overlooking the south lawn to the railroad tracks beyond. Opposite, above: The restoration of La Posada's artistic and elegant soul is one of the great success stories of Route 66. Opposite, below: The piano in the ballroom of La Posada, where guests are sometimes treated to an impromptu concert.

Fred Harvey and Mary Colter

Fred Harvey did more to civilize the West than anyone with a six-shooter. In a time when train travel meant going days without decent food, Harvey established lunch counters and dining rooms known for cleanliness and prompt service along the Santa Fe Railway line. He even came up with the crazy notion of hiring women. Well-trained young women worked in the eateries and became known as "Harvey Girls."

The Fred Harvey Company built hotels at prominent locations along the Santa Fe line. Some of the best known Harvey Houses were El Tovar and Bright Angel Lodge at the Grand Canyon. But La Posada was the most spectacular of all. Harvey's chief architect, Mary Colter, based the design of La Posada on the great haciendas of the Southwest. As with all her work, even when new the hotel looked gracefully aged, as if it had been there forever. La Posada was the only project for which Colter was able to design the buildings, decorate the interiors, and plan the gardens. She considered it her masterpiece.

ARIZONA HISTORICAL SOCIETY, FLAGSTAFF

ARIZONA MOMENT

Piano music wafts through the building.

It flows through the corridors, rises to the high ceilings, and curls up the spiral staircase. I am sprawled across my bed in La Posada. I should turn on my computer and get to work but instead I'm held hostage by a slow-spinning ceiling fan. Music floods the room, full and lush; juicy as field melon. Entranced, I listen to one song, another, and then another. Two verses in, I leap to my feet. Despite the orchestral leanings of the melody, I recognize the tune.

I scurry downstairs to the elegant ballroom filled with handcrafted furniture and bold artworks. Sunlight streams through French doors swung open wide. The sound is sharper here, soaring and defiant. I notice people amid the gardens, peering inside. I plop down on a sofa; all thoughts of work snatched from my head, and listen to 17-year-old Dan Terner play a joyous rendition of "Friend of the Devil" by the Grateful Dead.

Somewhere, Mary Colter—who lived long enough to see La Posada turned into office space—dances a jig.

Standin' on the Corner Park

La Posada became one of the great success stories of Route 66 and marked the beginning of a long, slow Winslow revival. Next up Winslow cashed in on its pop culture fame. They took an offhand mention in an Eagles' song and ran with it.

A life-size bronze statue of a young troubadour holding his guitar stands on a corner downtown. In the mural behind him a woman in a red pickup truck flashes the flirty eye. And visitors from all over the world stop to insert themselves into this little musical scenario. They pose with the statue—so many that his shoulders and backside are rubbed shiny—and snap a photo. There they are, standin' on a corner in Winslow, Arizona, such a fine sight to see. Now it feels like they've driven Route 66.

Downtown

After you finish standing on the corner, stand in a place where you can glean some sense of the history of the town. Old Trails Museum houses a bounty of exhibits that belie their limited space. Displays include Native American pottery, railroad artifacts, Route 66

Left: The giant wooden totem was carved by Peter "Wolf" Toth to honor Native Americans. *Above:* Winslow Visitor Center occupies one of the historic trading posts of the Hubbell empire. *Right:* Old Trails Museum represents the best of small-town museums; excellent displays in an accessible space.

memorabilia, and a seriously impressive collection of fossils, many of them discovered and donated through the years by a local bus driver who has a knack for archeology.

They restored a Hubbell Trading Post, the main distribution center for the Hubbell empire, to serve as a very cool visitor center, preserving many of the historic features, like the original floor scale and receiving desk.

Winslow tackled the weed-choked fringes along the railroad tracks and turned it into First Street Parkway, with a landscaped walking path winding past rail cars on display, benches, a bandstand, and a large, lanky Indian head. The wooden sculpture was carved by Peter Toth as part of his "Trail of the Whispering Giants." Toth created these totems for every state and chose Winslow as the proper setting for his Arizona sculpture.

Some other places worth checking out in Winslow are: Homolovi State Park, site of ancestral Hopi villages; McHood Park and Clear Creek, a popular swimming, fishing, and kayaking spot; Remembrance Garden, displaying salvaged beams from the Twin Towers of the World Trade Center.

Meteor City

At one time there were six trading posts between Winslow and Winona, but only Meteor City (Exit 239) reopened. Since 1979, the trading post has been housed in a hulking geodesic dome. The first dome burned in '90, but a new one was built a year later. The lofty ceiling soars overhead. Everything here is oversized. The World's Longest Map of Route 66 is splashed across panels of a plywood fence, and beside the frontage road stands a massive dreamcatcher. Appropriate, with so many dreams being chased down this highway.

Above: A dusky summer evening wafts through the massive dreamcatcher at Meteor City Trading Post. *Below:* You never have to worry about getting lost at Meteor City with the World's Longest Map of Route 66 on display.

Meteor Crater

Some attractions, like Meteor Crater (Exit 233), require no hype. Fifty thousand years ago a meteor screamed through the atmosphere and slammed into the high plateau, gouging out a vicious divot, 700 feet deep and 4,000 feet across. The explosion threw millions of tons of rock clear and resulted in hurricane-force winds. Things have since calmed down.

The main building perches on the rim of the crater and contains a gift shop, snack bar, and terrific interactive museum. Visitors can even use a computer simulation to make their

own crater, using meteors in small to apocalyptic sizes. An insightful short film runs in the auditorium. Outside viewing platforms are positioned on the rim and at lower levels. Guided tours are offered daily of this true natural wonder, the first proven and best preserved meteor impact site on earth.

Two Guns

Two Guns (Exit 230) sits on private land, so respect all signs and gates. If the site is accessible, browse among the picturesque ruins that teeter on the rocky edge of Canyon Diablo. The original trading post and roadside zoo dates back to the '20s. Still visible is the Apache Death Cave, where 42 Apache raiders were burned to death in a violent confrontation with Navajos in 1882. Multiple alignments of Route 66 crisscross the scarred ground and the 1914 reinforced concrete bridge spans the bloody canyon.

Top: Meteor Crater is nearly a mile across and 2.4 miles around the top.
Above and right: The ghost town of Two Guns, with its sprawling ruins, is well worth a visit by curious travelers.
Opposite: The ruins of Meteor Crater Observatory retain a certain forlorn dignity despite the ravages of time.

Twin Arrows

Although the Twin Arrows Trading Post (Exit 219) remains closed, the giant arrows were restored in 2009 thanks to the work of preservation-minded groups. Across the interstate, the Navajo Nation plans to open a hotel and casino.

Right: The Winona Trading Post is now a modern gas station and store. *Below:* The history of Route 66 is being saved bit by bit, like Twin Arrows, rebuilt and repainted in 2009.

Winona

Better than oversize arrows, domes, or holes, Winona has a bulletproof roadside attraction: song lyrics that stick in your head. Three words in Bobby Troup's little ditty—"Don't forget Winona"—and a Route 66 legend was born. The reality is Winona (Exit 211) started as a station on the railroad and never progressed much beyond that.

Yet Winona marks a dramatic shift of the landscape. After miles of sparse sun-scorched plateaus, Winona reintroduces you to the simple pleasure of trees. A few junipers begin appearing near Twin Arrows, but Winona trots out the big timber, the ponderosa pines, forming the edge of an expansive forest.

Continue on Townsend-Winona Road, the original Route 66 alignment, for 10 miles. You'll pass farm fields and grassy meadows, streaked summer-to-frost with wildflowers. A 1924 steel truss bridge no longer handles traffic but sits on a short stretch of abandoned roadbed. The road curves through pine-scented woods, with snatches of the San Francisco Peaks framed at every break in the trees. Once you reach the stoplight at U.S. 89, turn left into Flagstaff.

Better than oversize arrows, domes, or holes, Winona has a bulletproof roadside attraction: song lyrics that stick in your head.

Top: Built in 1914, the Padre Canyon Bridge can be reached only by 4WD vehicle.
Above: The steel arch of the 1924 Winona Bridge frames the San Francisco Peaks.

CHAPTER 5

Flagstaff

ROUTE 66'S BACKYARD

NORTHERN ARIZONA UNIVERSITY, CLINE LIBRARY

Opposite: Nestled at the foot of the San Francisco Peaks and surrounded by national forest, Flagstaff is Route 66 Arizona's backyard.

Above: Route 66 and Santa Fe Avenue in 1958.

Nestled at the foot of the San Francisco Peaks, Flagstaff maintains a rhythm all its own. The town is a comfortable mix of college students, ski bums, climbers, bikers, hikers, professors, and ranchers.

Hearty but laid-back; funky but with an undertow of culture, Flagstaff sits amid pine-clad hills at 7,000 feet above sea level, giving it that mountain town swagger. These are healthy people who live outdoors and exist on thimblefuls of oxygen. And they all have long-limbed dogs that lope at their side, with Frisbees dangling from slobbery, happy mouths.

Trails for hiking and biking vein the surrounding slopes. Three national monuments—Walnut Canyon, Sunset Crater, and Wupatki—lie on the outskirts. Flagstaff's play area stretches towards the Grand Canyon to the north and south into Oak Creek Canyon and the red rocks of Sedona.

Such a crescendo of competition keeps Flagstaff less focused on the beautiful stretch of Route 66 that rambles through the community on the shoulder of the railroad track. Too bad. Vintage motor courts and cafes dot the eastern segment of the Ma Road heading towards downtown.

fun fact

The San Francisco Peaks are part of a volcanic mountain range seven miles north of Flagstaff. The highest summit, Humphreys Peak, soars to 12,633 feet, the tallest mountain in Arizona.

Museum Club

If the term "roadhouse" didn't exist, someone would coin it for the Museum Club. This cavernous honky-tonk, fashioned as a giant log cabin, looms on the side of Route 66. It was built by a taxidermist in 1931 to house his immense collection of stuffed animals and weapons. Today, he would have his own reality show.

It was later turned into a nightclub. Don Scott then put the Museum Club on the map as a country music showcase. After buying it in the '60s, Scott, who had played with Bob Wills and the Texas Playboys, enticed big-name stars to perform.

Sadly, Scott's ownership ended in tragedy. His wife Thorna tumbled down the stairs and died in 1973. Shattered by the loss, Scott took his own life in the saloon two years later. Their spirits are said to haunt the Museum Club.

Miz Zip's

"Easy as pie" is one of the most perplexing idioms of the English language. There's nothing easy about preparing pie. Most homemade food requires work and patience. Yet at Miz Zip's, that's the only way they know how to do things. Fries are fresh cut and they butcher their own meats. This comfy diner is exactly the type of place you hope to find in every town and seldom do.

Pies alternate daily, depending on the whim of the pie maker and what's fresh. I ordered peach, not a slice so much as a slab, mounds of sunshine-hued fruit cradled by delicate crust. That joyous collision between peach pie and vanilla ice cream is like biting into summer itself.

"We just try to make good food and our customers seem to appreciate it," says owner Judy Leonard. "They keep coming back anyway."

Easy as pie.

———

Above: Built around five large ponderosa pines, the Museum Club has a tree in the middle of the dance floor. *Left:* Some diners strive for a retro feel and some, like Miz Zip's, just keep doing what they've always done, decade after decade. Waitress Haylee McElroy serves coffee with a smile.

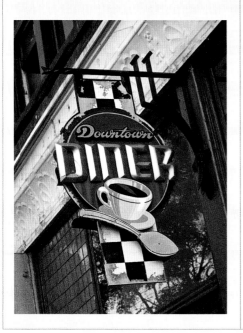

fun fact

According to Jackson Browne, the idea for the song "Take It Easy" began not on a corner in Winslow, but in Flagstaff, when he saw a girl pulling out of Der Wienerschnitzel. And she wasn't driving a flatbed Ford but a Toyota. Der Wienerschnitzel is now Route 66 Dog Haus.

Downtown

Flag, as it's known around the state, pulls off a dandy trick, managing to feel hip and historic at the same time. Bars, restaurants, galleries, and shops fill the graceful Victorian and Tudor-revival buildings, many dating back to the 1880s. Anchoring the bustling downtown are two stately dames, Hotel Weatherford and Hotel Monte Vista. Both boast storied pasts, long lines of celebrity guests, and ghosts aplenty.

The 1927 Santa Fe depot houses the visitor center and also the Amtrak station. Trains rumble through the heart of town day and night, adding a touch of urban sophistication but occasionally necessitating the use of earplugs for those overnighting near the tracks.

Clockwise, from top: Trains still rumble through Flagstaff on a daily basis. The old Santa Fe Depot now houses the Amtrak Station and a visitor center. • Route 66 and the railroad are forever entwined, both following the path forged by the Beale Expedition. • Downtown Flagstaff is a vibrant blend of shops, galleries, and eateries housed in historic buildings.

NORTHERN ARIZONA UNIVERSITY, CLINE LIBRARY

Haunted Hotel

For sheer number and diversity the roster of ghosts at Hotel Monte Vista stacks up with anyone. Even no-nonsense John Wayne once spotted a spook at Monte V. A crying baby often chases workers from the basement. A woman rocks by the window in room 305, murdered prostitutes waken guests with chilling glares in 306, the phantom bellboy (seen by Wayne) knocks on doors and declares "room service" in muffled tones, and my favorite, the bank robber.

As the story goes, in 1970 three men robbed a bank and stopped by the Monte Vista lounge despite one being shot during the getaway. While toasting newfound wealth, the wounded man died. Now numerous bar patrons report being greeted by a cheery disembodied voice proclaiming, "Good morning."

I love that optimism. Here's a guy who made mistakes, sure. Yet his spirit seems content. He doesn't menace, doesn't make bottles fly around the room. He just delivers a jolly salutation and lingers, as if hoping somebody will buy one last round.

Opposite: A young Arizona Cardinals fan, Parks Adams, checks out the downtown scene in Flagstaff. *Above:* The Hotel Monte Vista today and in 1945. *Left:* Room 306 is said to be haunted by two murdered prostitutes.

Lowell Observatory

Anybody who took 6th-grade science knows two things. First, Uranus is pronounced in a way that makes it sound like you're talking about your butt. Giggling ensues. And second, Pluto is a planet. Period.

Lowell Observatory was established in 1894, making it one of the oldest observatories in the country. Founder Percival Lowell believed he discovered evidence of life on Mars from this high perch. His conclusions intensified the interest in space and may have led to author H. G. Wells publishing his novel *War of the Worlds* a few years later. In 1930 Clyde Tombaugh discovered the planet Pluto from Lowell. In recent years Pluto has been kicked to the curb by solar system bigwigs, meriting only "dwarf planet" status. Sixth graders know better.

Visitors can watch multimedia shows in the auditorium, travel the universe in the 3D space theatre, take a guided tour, and view the sun through a specially equipped telescope. At night, you'll have a chance to discover planets of your

own while peering through the original 24-inch Clark telescope Percival Lowell once used to study the landscape of Mars. If Uranus appears, expect giggling.

Galaxy Diner

When it comes to blasts from the past, the Galaxy fires both barrels. The joint is wreathed in a halo of neon. The menu covers expected ground and then some. Burgers are chopped steak and fries are cooked twice, and you can get them "wet," meaning slathered with gravy. The Galaxy also functions as a sort of retro community center, with a car show every Friday night and free swing dance lessons on Saturday.

Arboretum of Flagstaff

Spread across 200 acres and sheltered by towering ponderosa pines, the Arboretum of Flagstaff is a botanical garden, nature center, and scientific research station tucked away in a beautiful corner of the Coconino National Forest. Trails wind through shady gardens, past open meadows and along cool creeks and ponds.

Over 2,500 species of plants can be found at the Arboretum, most divided into themed gardens. Abundance captures

your attention, the sheer diversity of plant life, spilling from beds and crowding pathways. Unlike some botanical facilities that tend to be more formalized, a gentle shagginess permeates the Arboretum. Gardens flow from one to the next and diffuse plantings blend together in a relaxed natural setting. Gravel paths meander through a forest so enchanted that a gaggle of dwarves singing "Hi ho, hi ho" wouldn't seem out of place.

Rejoin I-40 at Exit 191.

Top: Pluto was the only planet (or dwarf planet) discovered from a high perch above Route 66, Lowell Observatory. *Above:* Along the Arboetum's shady nature trails, you might see a swallowtail butterfly, Arizona's state butterfly, visiting the wildflowers. *Left:* Plenty of classic tunes on the jukebox keep the joint jumping at Galaxy Diner. *Opposite:* A local car club meets at the Galaxy Diner every Friday night, blending hot rods and cool neon.

Left: Plenty of old fashioned swimming holes can be found in Oak Creek, like this spot above Slide Rock State Park. *Opposite:* Cathedral Rock, one of Sedona's most famous formations, turns incandescent in the late-day sun.

SIDE TRIP

Sedona Swimming Holes

People flock to the Sedona area for many reasons, most notably the jaw-dropping red rock scenery. Others are on a spiritual quest, crouching at vortexes to listen to the earth hum. Or they come for art galleries or world-class spas. Yet some have a simpler agenda. They come to get wet.

This portion of Arizona harbors a collection of truly unforgettable swimming holes. Streams tumble from the high country of the Colorado Plateau, carving dramatic canyons, such as Sycamore, Wet Beaver, and the most spectacular of all, Oak Creek Canyon, the slender red rock gorge connecting Flagstaff and Sedona.

The drive on State Route 89A through Oak Creek Canyon is a stunning visual feast. The first few miles travel through a forest of ponderosa pines. This is window-down driving. The perfume of warm pine must be what heaven smells like on laundry day. From the lip of the Mogollon Rim the road drops in a series of switchbacks to the canyon floor where it traces the silver thread of the stream, amid woodlands luscious and intimate. The liquid dagger of the creek carves out the details and sings this canyon to life.

One of the best-known swimming holes in the entire Southwest is Slide Rock State Park, seven miles north of Sedona. In what once was a thriving apple orchard, stone banks throttle the creek into a narrow frothy chute, creating a natural water ride. Along the route are pools of varying depths, perfect for wading, swimming, and cliff jumping.

Kids and grown-ups ping-pong through the chute on summer days. Word of warning: Wear cut-offs or other sturdy shorts. Adults may scrape bottom through the shallows, so it's not uncommon to stand up at the end of the slide, only to see swatches of your delicate bathing suit continue downstream.

Next up is Grasshopper Point, a more tranquil nook located two miles north of Sedona. Bracketed by small, feisty waterfalls and guarded by a clutch of graceful Arizona sycamores, the stream gathers in a blue-green pool 50 feet wide at the base of a terraced cliff. Swimmers can make a straight plummet into deep water from heights of 5, 10, and 20 feet.

With afternoon waning, you have time to drive through Sedona to Crescent Moon Picnic Area, better known as Red Rock Crossing. There you'll step into a postcard. Cathedral Rock reflected in the waters of Oak Creek is one of the most photographed scenes in the state. So, while this iconic spot also draws crowds, they are spread over a wide area.

The shallow stream meanders past the base of Cathedral Rock and through forested groves. The bottom drops in a few places, forming nice pools. There's a rope swing upstream from Cathedral. While doing your best Tarzan impression from the swing you might notice the opposite bank covered with dozens of stacked rock totems, looking like a miniature Stonehenge. This is Buddha Beach, considered to be the site of a powerful vortex. Believers come to meditate, chant, and apparently, stack rocks.

Sedona exists at an impossible intersection of soul-nourishing wilderness and pampered luxury— where soaring red rock monoliths cradle an array of resorts, spas, art galleries, and boutique wineries. If you have an extra day or two, they could hardly be better spent than exploring Sedona.

CHAPTER 6

Williams

A GRAND STRETCH

Old gas pumps are among the memorabilia found at Route 66 Roadhouse in Bellemont. *Opposite:* Of the Route 66 Arizona towns, Williams has best reclaimed past glory, and looks shiny and new, like this modified 1932 Ford Model A (background) and 1957 Chevy (foreground), at a car show during the Cool Country Cruise-in.

Flagstaff serves as a sort of midway point of Route 66 Arizona. While much of the eastern half is segmented and broken, that begins to change amid the big timber. From here on out the two-lane overpowers the superslab. It's mostly Route 66 between Flag and Williams, with some intriguing stops along the way.

Bellemont

There's not much to Bellemont (Exit 185) these days, but a cool scene from Easy Rider was filmed here. As Peter Fonda and Dennis Hopper pulled up in front of the Pine Breeze Motel, the door cracked open and the proprietor peered out to see motorcycles. Immediately the neon "NO" next to the "VACANCY" flickered to life. Today, the closed Pine Breeze offers bikers free camping and the infamous "NO VACANCY" sign is proudly displayed at the nearby Route 66

Roadhouse Bar & Grill, a bike-friendly saloon. Revenge is a dish best served with a cold beer.

Sitting across the street from a Harley Davidson dealership, the Route 66 Roadhouse pays homage to all things Harley. The table tops are glass-covered motorcycle wheels and a Harley Davidson jukebox keeps the beat grooving. They sell cuts of meat that customers can slap on the grill. The joint has three pool tables, six TVs, a free dartboard and big patio out back. Plus, there are 28 beers on tap and over 400 bottles of whiskey filling the back bar. Nobody walks out thirsty.

fun fact

The 65 mile segment of Route 66 from Brannigan Park to Parks is listed in the National Register of Historic Places.

Brannigan Park

If you're willing to travel some unpaved portions in exchange for heart-squeezing panoramas, cross to the north frontage road and continue west. The road hugs I-40 for a couple of miles before swinging northwest, now a 66 alignment. The pavement ends briefly as you proceed through Brannigan Park, where beautiful spring-fed meadows are framed by groves of pine and aspen. Auto Tour signs have been posted by the forest service and a couple of old Mother Road alignments have been preserved as shady walking paths.

As you cross a mountain pass you reach the highest point on Route 66, over 7,300 feet. Paving resumes and soon you're pulling into the historic general store at Parks.

Parks

Built in 1921, Parks Feed and Mercantile (Exit 178) predates Route 66 by five years. It still maintains an old-fashioned charm, even harboring the post office, while serving the needs of the community. Gas up and spend a few bucks for snacks if nothing else. These are businesses that deserve our support.

Grand Canyon Deer Farm

Open since 1969, Grand Canyon Deer Farm (Exit 171) is an elaborate petting zoo where visitors get up close and personal with the animals. Those with food cups are quickly immersed in a furry phalanx of gregarious deer. This is not the place for designer duds, since the critters regard clothing as chewing gum. Kids love the place! You'll also meet wallabies, llamas, pot-bellied pigs, mini-donkeys, camels, and plenty more.

After leaving the Deer Farm, you can return to the interstate or continue west on the old alignment, which becomes gravel and skirts Davenport Lake, a part-time body of water. Enter I-40 at Exit 167.

Williams

Of all Route 66 burgs, Williams (Exit 165) has done the best job of recapturing its pre-interstate vibrancy. The town jumps all summer long. Historic buildings are strung along a few blocks of a divided Route 66, a nice mix of eateries, saloons, and trading posts. Crowds duck in and out of shops that stay open late. Stores staying open in the evening may not seem like much, but it's huge in a small town.

Nighttime streets are splashy with neon. Music from street-side patios drifts up and down the boulevard, weaving together a road-friendly soundtrack. Horse-drawn carriages clop through downtown and crowds gather in a different spot each evening to watch the nightly gunfight. Just about every summer weekend is booked with some kind of festival, so don't be surprised to find the town jammed with classic cars, Harleys, rodeo riders, or the smoky aroma of barbecue, depending on what's on the calendar.

Above: Part museum, part gift shop, Pete's Route 66 Gas Station Museum is a tribute to old-time service stations. Pete's dad bought this Ford Custom new in 1950. *Left:* Grand Canyon Deer Farm introduces visitors to all sorts of critters, including Gracie the camel. *Opposite:* The beautiful patio of Cruiser's Café 66 sits right on the Mother Road and there's usually a guy with a guitar singing and meaty ribs sizzling on the grill.

It wasn't always like this. Williams struggled after the loss of Route 66 same as other towns, but they had an ace in the hole. A mighty big hole. The Grand Canyon lies 60 miles to the north and that was the cornerstone of their revival.

Grand Canyon Railway

The first railroad reached Grand Canyon in 1901 and revolutionized the Northern Arizona tourism business. Before this, getting to the Grand required a long kidney-pummeling stagecoach ride. Suddenly people could chug to the edge of the Big Ditch in comfort. But once Americans went gooey over automobiles, trains were all but forgotten. The spur line to the Grand ceased operation in '68 and sat rusting in the sun until Grand Canyon Railway restored the track, brought in vintage trains and began operation in '89.

Passengers depart from Williams and rumble through 65 miles of high plains and pine forests before arriving at Grand Canyon's historic log depot. They can spend the next few hours enjoying the sights before returning on the afternoon train, or check into one of the canyon hotels (with reservations, of course) and return on a different day. There are four classes of service to choose from aboard Grand Canyon Railway.

With a steady flow of visitors coming to Williams to ride the train, improvements began popping up slowly through the town.

Top: The Grand Canyon Railway played an essential role in reviving the town of Williams. *Above:* Conductor Ed Greer keeps things running smoothly aboard Grand Canyon Railway.

Bearizona

For animal lovers who don't want to peer through cages at wildlife, this facility solves that problem. You simply drive past the gates and into 158 acres of pine forest, populated with a diverse mix of burros, bison, Dall and bighorn sheep, bears, and more, all roaming freely. Of course, the bears are partitioned off from their snack-like neighbors.

The layout of the park provides excellent views to all corners of the habitat. Keep an eye peeled as you slowly motor through, since the big mammals are apt to shamble across the road in front of you. That's not the sort of thing that happens at zoos, but enjoying animals in a natural setting is the Bearizona experience. At the end of the three-mile drive, you'll reach Fort Bearizona, the walk-through area, populated by park babies. Playful bear cubs scramble up tree limbs and wolf pups furiously wrestle.

Right: The neon steer on the roof of Rod's Steak House has served as a beacon to hungry travelers since 1946.

Rod's Steak House

Anytime you see a neon-lit steer on the roof of a restaurant, it's a safe bet that tofu isn't on the menu. In 1946 Rodney Graves opened Rod's Steak House to a bustling business. In the post-war boom, Americans streamed west on Old Double Six and couldn't resist the enticement of a roof cow.

Lawrence Sanchez and his wife Stella purchased Rod's Steak House in 1985. Lawrence had washed dishes at Rod's as a teenager and returned to work as manager and chef. Aware of the steak house's storied history, the couple preserved the look and spirit of Rod's. The steer-shaped menu, now a registered trademark, is the same one Rod used to open the eatery. Many of the same recipes are used, including a sugar-dipped charred steak.

Above left: The drive-thru wildlife park of Bearizona is one of the newest and splashiest roadside attractions along Route 66.
Above right: Fort Bearizona is a walking portion of the park, where visitors get some up-close peeks at the resident babies.

SIDE TRIP

Grand Canyon

Here's a good rule of thumb. Any time you're an hour away from one of the Seven Natural Wonders of the World, make the drive. Don't hold out thinking maybe you'll pass closer to one of the other six natural wonders farther down the road.

Upon admission you'll receive a copy of the park's newspaper, *The Guide*, containing information, maps, shuttle schedules, program times,

and seasonal points of interest. Keep it handy. Park when you hit Grand Canyon Village. Free shuttle buses operate three color-coded routes. No tickets are required and bus stops are clearly marked.

Even couch potatoes can hike at the Grand Canyon. The easy Rim Trail serves as a thoroughfare for the Village, but it also stretches for miles in both directions, much of it paved and shaded. Once you're clear of the Village, crowds melt away and you can enjoy the canyon in solitude.

If you're remotely fit, hike below the rim for a revelatory experience.

Head down Bright Angel to Mile-and-a-Half Resthouse or South Kaibab to Cedar Ridge. Both are three-mile round-trips. Your knees might grumble, but your soul will thank you.

Anyone who spends time staring into the Earth's most gaping wound and doesn't have a few geology questions isn't paying attention. The exhibits at Yavapai Observation Station provide the answers and the expansive windows provide the views.

When Santa Fe Railway hired architect Mary Colter to design a gift shop and rest area in 1930 they definitely got their money's worth. The 70-foot stone-and-mortar tower of Desert View Watchtower proves to be one of Colter's most enduring and dramatic creations. Perched on a promontory at canyon's edge, the tower commands an unmatched view of the Painted Desert, San Francisco Peaks, and a long stretch of Colorado River. The interior walls feature murals by Hopi artist Fred Kabotie.

Looking for the best sunset viewing spot? Just step outside. Seriously. They range from magnificent to awesome. Hopi Point draws big crowds, so if you want some elbow room try Yaki, Pima, or Lipan Points.

PLANES OF FAME AIR MUSEUM

On your return from the canyon, be sure to stop at Valle Airport. There you'll find the Planes of Fame Air Museum. A cavernous hangar is filled to the rafters with beautifully restored antique planes, warbirds, models, munitions, and lots of classic cars. Outside you can tour the interior of the Lockheed C-121A used by General Douglas MacArthur.

After touring Planes of Fame, walk over to the terminal where the airport owner displays a private collection of antique aircraft and autos, including a 1906 Reo Runabout, a 1934 Ford Phaeton, and lots more. Valle Airport sits 30 miles north of Williams on State Route 64.

Above: Warbirds, antique and model planes, classic cars, and munitions fill the hangar of the Planes of Fame Air Museum. Opposite: Mary Colter designed Desert View Watchtower to resemble the architecture of the Puebloan people of the Colorado Plateau. Opposite below: The grand view from Yaki Point.

Twisters 50's Soda Fountain

Man does not live by pie alone. Sometimes creamy chocolate malts are needed, or old-timey root beer floats. With their black and white floor, shiny red booths, and walls plastered with vintage Coke signage, Twisters is so spot-on authentic you might catch a whiff of Potsie's Brylcreem. Besides the nostalgia, they also dish up some mighty fine grub.

Pine Country Restaurant

Pie is life's pause button. Things slow down for pie, making it or eating it. Plenty of desserts satisfy a sweet tooth, but only one is an institution. Cake is just a candle transportation system. Cookies are a way for Girl Scouts to shake us down. But pie … pie conjures images of warm kitchens, heady aromas, and someone in an apron. More than any other food, pie means love.

The Pine Country pie case is placed cunningly by the front door. Shelves are stacked with an array of colorful, almost majestic, creations. Luscious cream pies, plump fruit pies, and specialty numbers crowned with slabs of chocolate and gleaming berries.

"I wanted to do something to define the restaurant and I thought of pies," says owner Dee Seehorn. "People have a special connection to pies. You see it in their eyes when they walk through the door."

I dove face-first into a strawberry cream cheese, available only in summer. It arrived buried under an avalanche of berries and whipped cream and tasted even more delicious than it looked.

Gunfights

"A cowboy is shot down on the streets of Williams every day," boasts the city. The Cataract Creek Gang roams the streets beginning in late afternoon. They argue and exchange taunts, while cajoling passersby, thus laying the groundwork for their nightly summertime gunfight.

Twisters 50's Soda Fountain provides a cozy corner where Route 66 travelers can enjoy a burger and shake. *Right:* Eric Eikenberry, astride his iron steed, takes part in Williams' nightly gunfight as a member of the Cataract Creek Gang.

Reborn Lodging

GRAND CANYON HOTEL—If you're looking to step back in time without forsaking comfort, you can't go wrong at the Grand Canyon Hotel. It was built in 1891, making it the oldest hotel in Arizona, and restored with a loving touch by Oscar and Amy Fredrickson. The hotel offers 25 rooms full of old-fashioned charm. No televisions but spotlessly clean and stylishly decorated. Be sure to check out the hotel register on display from 1904, signed by John Muir, Black Jack Pershing, and the King of Siam.

RED GARTER BED AND BAKERY—This former brothel was part of Williams' famed Saloon Row before being expertly converted into a quaint, antique-filled inn. Comfortable as the rooms are, guests may have trouble sleeping late once the bed-emptying aroma of fresh pastries wafts upstairs from the first-floor bakery. John Holst recognized the historic value of Williams and turned this former house of tarts into a modern house of . . . well, tarts. Rooms are character-rich and Holst happily spins tales of the building's (and the town's) bawdy past.

THE LODGE ON ROUTE 66—Rob Samsky bought a condemned motor court and undertook an almost unimaginable rehabilitation project. Everything was gutted and restored, from the fixtures to the frame. The Lodge on Route 66 hearkens back to something that had long been missing from Williams: family-run luxury lodging. Guests are welcomed by amenities like travertine flooring and countertops, solid wood furniture and plush bedding. The exterior exudes a Southwestern feel with an open courtyard surrounding a lovely covered cabana. Rustic chairs are positioned along the walkway, creating an old-fashioned chat-with-your-fellow-travelers vibe.

Above: All sorts of historic treasures can be found on Route 66, including Grand Canyon Hotel, the oldest hotel in Arizona. *Left:* The Lodge on Route 66 offers a casual elegance while maintaining its funky motor court charm.

Ash Fork

West of Williams the big ponderosas scatter, replaced by junipers and hunched piñon pines. Dropping through the cut in Ash Fork Hill, a wide savannah sweeps the timber back onto distant slopes and views break open wide.

The former railroad town of Ash Fork (Exit 144) is known as the "Flagstone Capital of the U.S.A." Several flagstone yards ship locally quarried pieces all over the country. But since slabs of rock make unwieldy souvenirs, Ash Fork often gets overlooked. Make the stop anyway. The visitor center houses the lovely Ash Fork Route 66 Museum. The facility displays the history of the road, the railroad, and the region. It also features a deliciously detailed diorama of Ash Fork during its bustling heyday.

Ash Fork's museum is an absolute gem. Its detail-rich diorama (left and right) shows the town in its heyday.
Below: The flagstone of Ash Fork was originally quarried for the railroad to build bridges before growing into an industry all its own.

CHAPTER 7

Seligman

ADIOS TO INTERSTATE

Just west of Ash Fork it's time to give I-40 the brush. Sorry, Interstate, it's not you, it's me. You're great. You're fast, efficient, and reliable. You've taken me to wonderful places. But it's time for a break. I'm tired of sharing you with truck drivers and traveling salesmen. I'm tired of you telling me when I can stop to eat or use the can. I'm boss of my bladder.

I'm just not ready to rush into anything. I want to take it slow. I want to ramble. I want to amble. I may even decide to mosey and I don't need a semi crawling up my backside while I'm doing it. I want soft shoulders and more curves. I want seduction and the promise of what lies just ahead. I want to drive like a traveler, not a bat out of hell.

Crookton Road

The final break occurs at Crookton Road (Exit 139). There are no welcoming banners or informational kiosks at this quiet spot, but it is indeed a landmark. This is the beginning of the longest unbroken stretch of Route 66 still in existence, 158 miles all the way to the California border. Tires don't need to darken interstate pavement for the rest of the journey. This is the core of the Route 66 Arizona experience.

Hot rods, classic cars, muscle cars and clunkers all arrive in Seligman during the first weekend of May for the annual Fun Run. *Opposite:* Mother Road enthusiasts from all over the world make pilgrimages to Seligman, birthplace of Historic Route 66.

From the Crookton Road bridge transportation options fan out like the prongs of a trident. Railroad tracks form the middle prong, flanked by soulless I-40 and a thin familiar two-lane, all pointed west.

Route 66 curls into rolling hills and through a narrow pass. Almost immediately you're confronted by a poetic blast from the past: rows of recreated Burma Shave signs. For those too young to remember Burma Shave signs and their snappy bursts of random information, think of it as your grandparents' Twitter. After 17 miles you'll roll into Seligman, the birthplace of Historic Route 66.

Seligman

Seligman wouldn't exist without Route 66. And Historic Route 66 wouldn't exist without Seligman and a very prominent resident, Angel Delgadillo.

Back in the day, Angel Delgadillo was a barber in Seligman and his brother Juan ran the Snow Cap Drive-In. Business was good as traffic streamed through the middle of town on the Mother Road. That changed abruptly when the adjacent section of Interstate 40 opened and a deathly quiet fell over the town.

In 1987, Angel, along with Juan and other local business owners, formed the Historic Route 66 Association of Arizona and convinced the state to designate Route 66 a historic highway. Thus it began.

The first thing you notice about Angel Delgadillo is the perpetual smile, bright as neon. Then you spot the eye-twinkle and the warmth that infuses every handshake or pat on the shoulder. Next to Angel, Santa Claus seems surly.

Angel moves through his Route 66 gift shop in Seligman like a gentle whirlwind, signing autographs and throwing a lanky arm around folks who traveled thousands of miles just to have a photo taken with him. Not many retired small-town barbers command such admiration, but not many are credited with preserving a sweeping slice of American heritage.

"We were forgotten after the interstate opened and that was a sad time," says Angel. "Now people travel from all over the world just to visit us. Every day is a good day."

The first time I stopped in Seligman, I knew nothing about the history of the road or town. I watched tour buses unload hordes of folks speaking a litany of languages. They beelined into the barbershop. A group of motorcycles roared up and riders swung down, stiff from the journey. But instead of angling for the Black Cat Bar to cut the road dust with a cold beer, they made for the barbershop. Crowds that couldn't squeeze inside stood on the sidewalk, snapping photos through the window. Their excitement was palpable.

"Holy cow," I remember thinking. "Just how good is this barber?"

BARBER

ROUTE 66
Memorabilia

THE MOTHER ROAD

| CALIFORNIA US 66 | ARIZONA US 66 | NEW MEXICO US 66 | TEXAS US 66 | OKLAHOMA US 66 |

Get Your Kicks

Angel & Vilma's
Proudly Carry
Products

Made in the
USA

=GIFT
SHOP

Opposite: Angel Delgadillo, the small town barber who changed the world.
Left: Most days Angel Delgadillo holds court in his barbershop and the adjoining visitor center, signing autographs and spinning tales.

"We were forgotten after the interstate opened and that was a sad time," says Angel. "Now people travel from all over the world just to visit us. Every day is a good day."

fun fact

The Burma-Shave signs now dot the Route 66 landscape between Ash Fork and Kingman. Yet during the original ad campaign, Burma-Shave signs were not used in Arizona. Traffic was considered too sparse.

FUTURE
IN IT

Burma-Shave ®

TM AMERICAN SAFETY RAZOR

Snow Cap Drive-In

Juan Delgadillo, Angel's brother, built the Snow Cap Drive-In from scrap lumber he gathered while working for the railroad. The place opened in 1953 and quickly earned a wacky reputation because of Juan's interaction with the customers. Juan's freewheeling gags— like "accidentally" squirting patrons with mustard that's actually colored string and offering comically undersized and oversized servings—delighted families for decades. After Juan passed away in 2004, those traditions have been carried on by his kids. And just because the Delgadillos are quick with a joke doesn't mean they don't know how to cook. The burgers are so tender you wonder how they ever kept a cow upright.

Below: A 1959 Ford Edsel sits in front of The Rusty Bolt while attention-grabbing mannequins adorn the roof.
Opposite: Hospitality and darn good coffee have made Historic Seligman Sundries an essential stop for international travelers. A 1955 Chevrolet Handyman greets visitors.

Main Street

The passion for a two-lane ribbon of asphalt extends beyond the Delgadillos. Preservation has become the watchword in Seligman. While the town spreads over just a few blocks, that short stretch reveals a delicious slice of Americana. Memorabilia from shops spills out into the street, while painstakingly restored motels and cafes lure motorists with postcard-worthy signs.

Your first stop, as everyone's should be, is Delgadillo's Route 66 Gift Shop & Visitor Center, adjacent to Angel's barber shop. It is a pilgrimage. You'll likely have to elbow your way through a small mob, but it's worth it just to say thanks to the Mayor and his family. Next time you think one person can't change the world, remember Angel Delgadillo.

Another essential visit is Historic Seligman Sundries, housed in one of the oldest commercial buildings in town. Frank and Lynne Kocevar are part of the new generation of folks, following up on the work Angel and others started.

They've restored the old building, even preserving the vintage soda fountain. Old signs paper the walls and antiques line the shelves. Besides the souvenir selection, they are known for their gourmet coffee.

More importantly, they've created an international welcome center. Seems like everyone on the road passes through the store, and Frank and Lynne can tell you who's out and about on any given day. If you need to leave a message or pick up news, stop by Historic Seligman Sundries.

This should be the most American road trip of all, yet any business owner along Route 66 will tell you that the majority of people traveling the road hail from a different country. The Mother Road is an international icon. "Route 66 has come to symbolize the very best of America to people all around the world," says Frank Kocevar. "It means freedom and a sense of adventure, and that resonates with everyone, no matter what language they speak."

A burger is king of comfort food because it's a flashback on a bun, transporting us to simpler times at first bite. A visit to Snow Cap in Seligman is a reminder that life is delicious and should never be taken too seriously.

Westside Lilo's Café

Perched, as the name implies, on the west edge of Seligman, Lilo's serves up scratch-made food in plate-draping portions. Everything is big here, from the jaw-unhinging burgers to the cinnamon rolls the size of manhole covers. Which makes it a challenge to save room for pie, but it's a decision you won't regret.

Lilo Russell has been baking most of her life. Her carrot cake, made using her great-grandmother's recipe, is legendary. She makes an assortment of cream pies daily, using mascarpone cheese—the same cheese used in tiramisu—infusing them with a defiant silkiness. Unlike some cream pies that quiver and collapse at first touch of a fork, Lilo's are as luxurious in texture as they are in taste.

I opted for a slice of banana split cream pie, a riotous medley of flavors. The crunch of nuts, the melt-in-the-mouth banana and chocolate cream mixed with sweet berries and a zing of chocolate sprinkles stayed with me for miles down the road.

Fun Run

To celebrate the new Historic Route 66 dedication, Seligman kicked it off with a rolling party on wheels that has become an annual event. The Arizona Route 66 Fun Run takes place every year on the first weekend of May. Thousands of enthusiasts participate, many in classic cars and hot rods, to make the showy drive to Topock/Golden Shores. To register, contact Historic Route 66 Association of Arizona.

Top: Lilo Russell displays a photo of the Havasu Harvey House that once graced the town of Seligman. *Above left:* Westside Lilo's Café is known for baked goods. *Left:* Fun Run brings out the best examples of shiny iron. *Opposite:* The Route 66 Evening Cruise on the first night of Fun Run is a Seligman tradition.

CHAPTER 8

The Open Road

TWO LANES OF FREEDOM

Pop culture artifacts, such as this Elvis statuette, fill the shelves at Hackberry General Store. *Right:* A reminder in Truxton that the Beale Wagon road was the precursor to Route 66. *Opposite:* Curves ahead! Modern-day pin-up model Kathleen Raye, seated in a 1957 Corvette, looks like she belongs in a calendar.

From Seligman you boom through the sprawling Aubrey Valley, ringed by shadow-painted mountains. This is the definition of Route 66 Arizona: small towns, big country. A land cracked wide beneath a great beast of a sky. I was suddenly struck by the genius of dogs. I get it now! Head-out-the-window, ears and tongue flapping, nostrils aflame—it's the only way to travel. I want to hang my head out the window, to smell the perfume of this short-grass prairie. I yearn to bite the wind.

Visitors from all over the globe seek out Route 66 because of stretches like this; the freedom of wide open spaces, a road that flies like an arrow towards the heart of the horizon, the music of tires on pavement through untamed lands.

Grand Canyon Caverns

The road climbs into some shaggy junipers and soon you spot Grand Canyon Caverns. You know it's a classic roadside attraction because they decorate the property with giant dinosaurs.

The complex includes motel, restaurant, RV Park, and gift shop. Don't be misled by the kitschy trappings; the caverns are spectacular. Descend by elevator 21 stories underground to take a guided tour through an immense series of chambers and tunnels. Personable guides lead you through the dramatic depths of flowstone formations and walls glittering with selenite crystals. Stout-hearted guests can spend the night in the Cavern Suite, a hotel room 220 feet below the surface.

In 1927 a young woodcutter named Walter Peck was on his way to a poker game when he nearly fell into a hole. He returned the next day with his buddies to discover a massive cave. Peck bought the property, believing it to contain mineral wealth. When that proved false, he opened the cavern for tours. Visitors plunked down a quarter for the privilege of being lowered by rope 150 feet into a massive pitch black hole. A candle was included in the tour price.

Left: It's not really a roadside attraction unless there's a dinosaur on the premises. *Below:* Grand Canyon Caverns includes motel, restuarant, gift shop, and riding stables, but the focus remains on the splendid cave tours. *Bottom:* Roll your window down and turn your radio up; you're rambling across Arizona on Route 66.

ARIZONA MOMENT

"Freaks of any kind give me the willies." So says John Agar, who plays the doctor of a nameless Arizona town in the 1955 sci-fi film, *Tarantula*. The movie about a giant arachnid seems especially vivid since I am watching it in a cave, deep below ground. I'm swaddled in utter darkness, save for the flickering of a flat screen television. I am spending the night in the Cavern Suite, a hotel room in the bowels of Grand Canyon Caverns. Sitting on the couch in the inky stillness, drinking beer, and watching a giant spider wreak havoc. As a middle-aged man, I would be embarrassed for anyone to know how toe-curlingly happy I am at this moment.

Grand Canyon Caverns is a natural limestone cave, the largest dry caverns in the United States. Dry being the operative word. Dry caverns support no life. No bats, rats, or bugs. And no freakishly large spiders, so I am immune to the "willies" that plague Agar.

Those who spend the night at Grand Canyon Caverns generally do so in the above-ground motel. The Cavern Suite is a totally different experience. The room comes with amenities like mini-fridge, microwave, television, sofa, and two double beds. It is a comfortable platform room sitting amid a chamber 400 feet long by 200 feet wide beneath 70-foot ceilings. Guests receive a private tour and specially prepared dinner and breakfast served in the suite.

An attendant is stationed topside by the elevator during a guest's stay. Judging by the looks I received when I told people my plans, this isn't for everyone. But I find it incredibly peaceful, soothing, and crazy fun. I would enjoy a great night's sleep except I don't want to waste time slumbering. A film library is on hand, but since my tastes run to 50's sci-fi, I brought my own. My playlist for the evening goes *Tarantula*, *The Mole People*, and *Monolith Monsters*, where the rocks turn killer. The rocks . . . the rocks . . . they're all around me! AGGHH!

Above: Tour guide Stefani Johnstun relaxes in the Cavern Suite deep underground in Grand Canyon Caverns.

Route 66 in Peach Springs is also the access point for the only road that goes to the bottom of the Grand Canyon. Diamond Creek Road is the only place between Lee's Ferry and Lake Mead where you can drive to the Colorado River. A permit must be purchased at Hualapai Lodge and the 20-mile unpaved road should be attempted only in a high-clearance vehicle. Still, it is one of the more amazing facets of this journey. You head west on Route 66, hang a right, and end up at the BOTTOM of the Grand Canyon.

The Frontier Café

Truxton barely qualifies as a wide spot in the road, but that's all you need for pie. The Frontier Café, connected to the Frontier Motel, shows some wear. Stools at the counter are wobbly, but so was I after so many desserts. They make everything from scratch, including pie. I ordered coconut cream because it sounded decadently tropical in this sun-spanked outback. Plus, it's not a personal favorite so it would be easier to push away.

South Rim, the colors more muted. But visitors can do a couple of things at Grand Canyon West they can't do elsewhere. Hikers preparing to trek into Havasu Canyon with its blue-green waterfalls tumbling like liquid turquoise often bunk at Hualapai Lodge. The Hualapai River Runners offer the only single-day rafting trip in the Grand Canyon, a nice blend of flat water and big rapids with some side canyons to explore.

Above: The Hualapai Lodge serves as base camp for some intriguing Grand Canyon adventures.
Left: Nate Bahe performs a tribal dance during the Hualapai barbecue, held during Fun Run.
Below: A slice of homemade pie and a counter stool at the Frontier Café await hungry travelers.

Peach Springs

Back on the right side of the earth, the highway soon enters the Hualapai Reservation, and then descends through scrubby rangeland into the community of Peach Springs. Once a former watering stop for steam locomotives, Peach Springs now serves as administrative headquarters for the Hualapai Indian Nation. A cultural center features rotating art displays and historic exhibits. Since reservation land includes 108 miles of the Colorado River and Grand Canyon, Hualapai Lodge makes a base camp for some one-of-a-kind adventures.

The Hualapai portion of the Big Ditch is narrower than what you see at the

Keepers of the Wild

After leaving Truxton the road squeezes through Crozier Canyon and its oddly stacked boulders, as if the Flintstones were having a yard sale.

One of the heart-warming surprises tucked along Route 66 is Keepers of the Wild Nature Park in Valentine, a non-profit rescue sanctuary for more than 150 abused, neglected, and abandoned exotic animals. Anyone up on Route 66 history knows about the old roadside zoos, which were pretty awful for the beasts. So Keepers provides a nice bit of karma. Tigers, lions, wolves, leopards, monkeys, and many more lounge in roomy habitats spread across the rocky hillsides. Visitors can wander through on their own steam or take a guided tour and hear the stories. Either way you can feel good knowing your admission is keeping some hard-luck critters in chow.

My plan backfired at first bite. It was rich without being overly sweet and reminded me of a pie my grandmother once made for me. It's a memory that hadn't stirred for decades and it flooded back by the forkful. That is the power of pie. Or as owner Betty Sutherland came out from the kitchen to explain, "Pie is the universal language of happiness."

Above: During a six-week bike trip from Savannah, Georgia, to Santa Monica, California, a group of Overland teens take a break in Truxton. *Left:* For feel-good stories it's hard to top Keepers of the Wild, providing sanctuary for unwanted animals.

Hackberry

Just ahead, a raucous clutter of roadside memorabilia infuses Hackberry General Store with a ramshackle charm that can't be measured. Owners John and Kerry Pritchard have created a delicious time capsule in this desert outpost, a shrine for road junkies.

Out front, a sweet red 1957 Corvette sits beside antique pumps. This is considered the quintessential Route 66 touring car ever since Tod and Buz traveled the highway in search of adventure on the CBS television show, *Route 66*. Across the grounds a scattered array of rusted machinery teeters between ruin and redemption.

Inside, vintage signage and Route 66 artwork adorn the walls. Shelves are stacked with Route 66 merchandise. One room is decked out like an old diner. Maps, books, and posters are everywhere.

"I wanted to turn this back into the kind of place people remember," says John Pritchard. "I grew up with old stores and I wanted to hang on to that. It's just a lot of old junk I collected, but when you see someone walk in and stop dead with tears in their eyes, it makes it all worthwhile."

A few miles past Hackberry you leave Crozier Canyon and enter a broad plain. Here you begin the longest continuous curve on Route 66, a swooping 7 miles as the road enters the Hualapai Valley beyond the reach of the surrounding mountain ranges.

A couple of miles into the curve, you'll feel like you've reached a suburb of Easter Island. One of the newest and weirdest Route 66 attractions, a 14-foot tall green tiki head sits at the corner of 66 and Antares Road in front of the Kozy Corner Trailer Court. Giganticus Headicus is the work of artist Gregg Arnold who created it in 2003 because … well, why not? The not-so-jolly green giant might seem out of place elsewhere, but this is Route 66. Quirky is the coin of the realm.

If someone has the ability and means to build an eye-grabbing roadside attraction on Route 66, they're carrying on a proud tradition. Arnold would have been a sap NOT to construct the oversized noggin.

The curve straightens out and you'll pass through Valle Vista, a bedroom community that surrounds a surprisingly nice golf course. By then you're on the outskirts of Kingman.

Opposite: With his penchant for antiques and collectibles, John Pritchard turned Hackberry General Store into a Route 66 icon.

Above: In the soft blush of twilight, a 1929 Model A Ford at Hackberry General Store appears fleet and fierce, ready to face the road ahead.

Left: Among a collection of pop culture luminaries, including Marilyn Monroe, Route 66 is always the star at Hackberry General Store.

NORTHERN ARIZONA UNIVERSITY, CLINE LIBRARY

fun fact

Charles Bronson and Clayton Moore, better known as the Lone Ranger, trained at Kingman Army Airfield.

Kingman is one of the towns still finding its way back, looking to redefine itself in the age of the superslab. Historic motels and eateries flashing signs of dreamy neon are mingled with newer businesses along Route 66, which is also called Andy Devine Avenue, after the raspy-voiced actor who grew up here.

While Kingman's downtown claims over sixty buildings on the National Register of Historic Places, the vacancy rate remains high. They lack the compressed energy of Flagstaff or Williams. But that may be changing. Some quality restaurants have a foothold now and other eateries and shops are bound to follow.

Kingman Army Airfield Museum

On the eastern edge of Kingman you'll reach a stoplight—so many miles since the last one in Seligman you may not recognize it at first. Tucked away amid the industrial park clutter surrounding the airport you'll find remnants of one of the largest gunnery schools built during World War II. Here 36,000 men trained as gunners for the B-17 bomber, known as the Flying Fortress. Decommissioned after the war, the base became Storage Depot 41, where thousands of warbirds were rendered down to aluminum ingots. The Kingman Army Airfield Museum, housed in an original 1942 wooden hangar, preserves artifacts, maps, and photos from this important chapter of American history. The folks operate on shoestring budget but do a great job of displaying the goods.

Route 66 stretches across the chest of Kingman parallel to the railroad tracks.

Downtown Kingman

One essential stop is the Kingman Powerhouse in downtown. Built in 1907, the hulking concrete structure fueled the energy needs of the town and surrounding mines until being

Left: Route 66 served as a vital artery during WWII. The Kingman Army Airfield Museum preserves a piece of that heritage.
Above: The Sage Drive-In in 1958.

eclipsed by Hoover Dam. Today the Powerhouse serves as a visitor center as well as housing the Historic Route 66 Association of Arizona with their gift shop and the Route 66 Museum.

Allow plenty of time for the museum, a treasure trove of history, stories, and pop culture analysis of Old Double Six. One centerpiece exhibit is a life-size model of a Dust Bowl–era family and overloaded truck as they prepare their meager evening meal. On the adjacent walls are poignant passages from John Steinbeck's *Grapes of Wrath*. The admission fee also includes a visit to the nearby Mohave Museum of History and

Arts, a delightful facility that includes a restored railroad caboose that was bound for the Smithsonian until gutsy little Mohave wrangled it away.

Kingman started out as a railroad town and it doesn't forget its heritage. Steam engine #3759 now resides beneath shady trees across the street from the Powerhouse, in Locomotive Park.

Visitors can climb aboard the big iron horse, the last steam engine to travel the rails between Chicago and Los Angeles.

Above: Exhibits at the Route 66 Museum depict the historical evolution of travel. *Left:* The Kingman Powerhouse includes a visitor center, the Route 66 Museum, and the offices and gift shop of Historic Route 66 Association. *Below:* The Hill Top Motel, a mid-century classic motor court, occupies a high perch away from the rumble of trains.

Mr. D'z Route 66 Diner

The eye-catching turquoise and pink color scheme and retro vibe pulls in the crowds at Mr. D'z. Even Oprah Winfrey once stopped for lunch and loved the homemade root beer so much, she gave cases of it away on her show. Breakfast is served all day, which should be a requirement for all diners. Root beer comes in frosted mugs and teases the tongue with a creamy caramel note.

Redneck's Southern Pit BBQ

Maybe you think you've had lemon pie before but you've only had imposters. The Ultimate Frozen Lemon Pie is a towering stack of creamy lemon goodness that arrives like plated sunshine. Tammy Floyd combined two family recipes and injected touches of her own to create a pie with the firmness of cheesecake yet that melts on my tongue like gelato.

Beyond the graham cracker crust, all resemblance to other lemon pies is purely coincidental. Meringue would be blasphemy. There is no gelatin base. The pie is formed in three distinct layers, with a fine bit of tartness at the bottom, fluffy lemon-rich layers floating above and topped with whipped cream and graham cracker sprinkles. At each bite, the pie melts into luxurious puddles allowing the lemon flavor to just hang

there, hugging my taste buds. Scratch-made food is a Floyd family tradition. Tammy's husband, Bubba, slow cooks a down-home Memphis-style barbecue over hickory wood fires. Dig in, just save room for pie.

Good eats are to be had at Mr D'z Route 66 Diner and Redneck's Southern Pit BBQ. *Right:* Shawna Andersen (left) and Brandi Pallerito dish up the grub at Mr. D'z. *Opposite:* The soft knife of neon carves the Route 66 night into rainbow-hued chunks that shimmer and seduce.

CHAPTER 9

Oatman

THE GOLDEN ROAD

The twisted, curving segment of Route 66 through the Black Mountains makes Oatman a popular destination with bikers. *Opposite:* It's a burro's world; we just live in it.

West of Kingman, Route 66 curls through the business edges, paralleling train tracks before crossing under Interstate 40. A scattering of homes and ranchettes dot the landscape but soon are a wisp in the rearview as the road streaks across an expanse of creosote-dotted sand flats.

Cool Springs Camp

After 20 miles, you'll reach another of the delicious success stories of Route 66 revival, Cool Springs Camp. Nestled in the shadow of Thimble Butte, Cool Springs was a gas station built in 1926 and later expanded to include tourist cabins. Traffic dwindled with the interstate and in '66 the camp burned down, leaving only two stone pillars and a foundation.

"When I first visited the ruins it looked like a place you'd take a guy to bump him off," says Ned Leuchtner. "But I was still intrigued. It was like hearing a voice telling me I was supposed to do something with this place. It began a journey."

After years of trying, Leuchtner was able to buy Cool Springs in 2001. Following a massive cleanup he utilized old photos to recreate the station and tourist camp in strikingly precise detail.

"This was an opportunity to preserve a piece of history and chances like that don't come along very often," says Leuchtner.

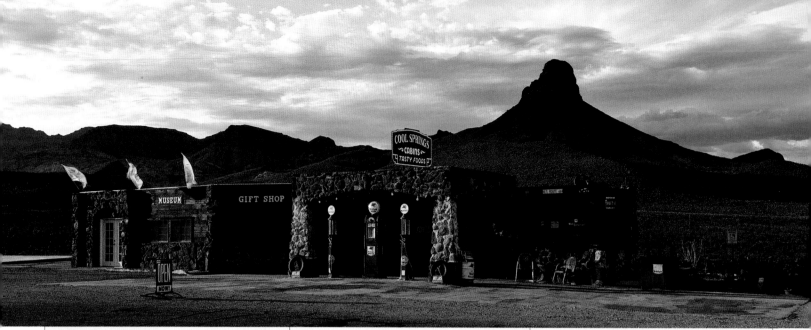

Today, Cool Springs operates as a gift shop, snack bar, and museum. More importantly, it occupies one of the most breathtaking and culturally significant pieces of the Mother Road. Cool Springs sits on the raggedy edge of nowhere. Perched on the cusp of a canyon, poised between the desert floor and the harsh fringe of the Black Mountains, Cool Springs provided a welcome oasis amid those brutal hills that boiled the radiators and broke the hearts of Okies.

From here the road careens up the mountainside in a torturous ascent. The next few miles are arguably the most scenic section of all Route 66. As you climb towards Sitgreaves Pass, toothy, broken country shambles away in all directions. The Blacks are a convulsed jumble of volcanic remains, spiny with Joshua trees, cacti, and yuccas. This series of hairpin curves and steep drop-offs so intimidated early travelers that many hired locals to drive their cars up the grade (the steepest on Route 66) or had them towed to the summit.

About a mile shy of the pass, watch for a flight of ghost steps carved from the rocky hillside. These lead up to Shaffer Fish Bowl Spring, a natural spring that collects in a concrete bowl and is often stocked with a few goldfish. It's also a popular watering spot for wild burros.

Pull over at the pass to let the blood rush back to your white knuckles. Take a minute to soak in devastating views that stretch into California and Nevada. The road writhes down through lava-capped hills for another three miles past the still operational Gold Road Mine into Oatman.

Oatman

Oatman hunkers in a craggy gulch, a once booming gold mining town, eight miles from Cool Springs. When the mines shuttered, the stream of traffic along Route 66 kept Oatman alive. A realignment in 1952 swung Route 66 south through Yucca, and Oatman teetered. But the growth of Laughlin and rebirth of Route 66 helped the town rebrand itself as a fun, funky destination.

A herd of burros from the surrounding hills wanders into Oatman daily. They loiter in the street, blocking traffic while mooching carrots (on sale in most shops) from tourists. The burros are descendents of animals used by area miners and abandoned when the mines closed. Like Oatman itself, the burros learned how to overcome adversity. When life hands you lemons, bray loudly until life forks over some crunchy carrots.

Covered sidewalks, plank floors, and corrugated tin walls lend an authentic Old West feel to the town. Start at the Oatman Hotel, built in 1902. This adobe structure no longer rents rooms but that doesn't mean they're unoccupied. A handful of ghosts are said to linger still, including two celebrities.

According to local legend, Clark Gable and Carole Lombard spent their wedding night in Room 15 of the hotel after marrying in Kingman in 1939. Although the story has been disputed, rumor has them returning to the hotel on several occasions. The marriage was cut tragically short when Lombard died in a plane crash in '42. Over the years, whispering and laughter have been reported emanating from the room. Perhaps the spirits of the screen legends returned to where they had been the happiest. The hotel maintains the upstairs as a museum.

Above: For visitors crossing the Mohave Desert, the sight of Cool Springs is as welcome today as it was in years past.
Left: The water in the Shaffer Fish Bowl saved many an overheated radiator.

London Bridge, Lake Havasu City

We all dream of spotting a treasure at a yard sale. We hope to take home one great bargain to discover it's worth a fortune. That's essentially the story of Lake Havasu City.

In 1963, Robert P. McCulloch, Sr., who had done well manufacturing chainsaws, purchased a 26-square-mile parcel of stark desert along the east shore of Lake Havasu. He asked his friend, C. V. Wood, the designer of Disneyland, to plan and build Lake Havasu City.

The town might have remained just another sleepy retirement community except that traffic increased halfway around the planet, and that made all the difference. In England, the venerable London Bridge was sinking into the Thames River due to busy city traffic. Rather than demolish the 136-year-old bridge, it was put up for sale. In 1968 McCulloch bought the world's largest antique for $2.46 million. The structure was dismantled and each of the 10,276 granite blocks were numbered and shipped to Long Beach, California. From there they were trucked inland and painstakingly reassembled. The deal also included ornate lampposts said to have been made from Napoleon's cannons captured at Waterloo.

It took three years and in October 1971, a dedication ceremony welcomed the bridge to its new home. The historic span connects the mainland with an island known as Pittsburgh Point. It is used by vehicles, pedestrians, and even Segway riders. Yes, the London Bridge that stood in the time of Charles Dickens, and that still bears strafing scars of Nazi warplanes, is the centerpiece of popular Segway tours. What a long, strange trip it's been.

fun fact

Every Fourth of July, Oatman hosts a Sidewalk Egg Fry.

Even more unusual is the sprawl of legal tender covering the walls of the hotel restaurant. Thousands of dollar bills are tacked up, a custom begun during the town's boom years. "Miners used to come in on payday and post a dollar. That would buy a lot of nickel beer," says Susie Clark, general manager of the Oatman Hotel. "They would drink until they got paid again or until their money ran out. It's just something that continued. People from all over the world write their name on a dollar and stick it on the wall. They come back to visit their money years later. We never take any down. It belongs to the people who put it up."

When you notice folks clustering in the street without a ravenous burro in the middle, it signals an impending gunfight. Gunfighter groups stage shootouts in the middle of Route 66 daily. The desperadoes work the crowd with practiced ease, paying special attention to the little pardners.

Leaving Oatman, the road weaves through lean and savage desert. It brushes past sharp-slanted mountains jutting in all directions as if the tectonic plates didn't just shift but engaged in a sultry bump and grind. The land is scraped to the marrow.

Languid curves bend past graveled hillsides freckled with creosote and groves of teddy bear cholla, the most insidious cactus in the desert. The plant is so spine-covered it appears fuzzy, yet each thorny pad breaks off at a whisper of movement. So prone to latch on to anyone who gets near them, they're often called "jumping cholla." Yet they can be absolutely dazzling, catching the sweet light at dawn and dusk and radiating a shimmering aura from golden spines.

The basin widens and flattens and goes to sand. Soon you arrive in the bedroom community of Golden Shores, with a few businesses scattered about. The road continues for five more miles,

dipping beneath the scraggly shade of salt cedars littering the marshes around Topock, which exists only as a name; the town is long gone. You skirt a backwater channel of Havasu National Wildlife Refuge then cross under a railroad overpass and that's the end of the line for Route 66 Arizona. The longest unbroken stretch of Route 66 ends as quietly as it begins.

Arching towards the saw-toothed mountains beyond, the Old Trails Bridge spans the Colorado River in one long, elegant crescent. An engineering marvel in 1916, the bridge no longer carries traffic, but a natural gas pipeline.

The mighty Colorado River coursing its way south to Mexico forms the West Coast of Arizona and the end of our journey.

Above: Between the antics of burros and daily gunfights, Oatman keeps visitors entertained. *Below:* The Colorado River marks the western boundary for Route 66 Arizona.

MOHAVE MUSEUM OF HISTORY & ARTS

ARIZONA
66
**ARIZONA
MOMENT**

I'm sitting on an exposed slab of stone atop the mesa overlooking Cool Springs Camp. I am a few hundred feet above Cool Springs, above Route 66. A hiking trail switchbacks up through the gaunt desert to the top of this promontory and views sweep across rocky ridgelines that gnaw the clouds with broken teeth.

I wear the late day silence like velvet as I gaze at the twisted ribbon below—this loopy, swoopy highway; this python of pavement; this mother of all roads—curling from the desert into ferocious hills. It is one of those profound "I Wonder" moments.

I wonder what everybody else on earth is doing right now. Not that it matters, I wouldn't trade places with anyone. I am exactly where I want to be.

People who consider roads inanimate are wrong. How can something without pulse seduce us? How can a breathless thing give us back pieces of our youth and create moments we'll cherish forever? Roads—some roads—are creatures fiercely alive.

The sun dips below the mountains and the sky turns—I suddenly notice—as golden as pie crust.

Cool Springs as it appeared in 1940, before it burned down and was later reborn. *Above:* The enticing curves of Route 66 flow westward out of the Black Mountains, towards the Colorado River.

WEST

**HISTORIC
US
66**

The Supai Motel in Seligman.

Places to See Along Arizona's Route 66

Navajo Nation

Yellowhorse Trading Post
854 Grant Road, Lupton, AZ 86508
(928) 688-2463, www.yellowhorseltd.com

Painted Cliffs Welcome Center
Interstate 40, Exit 359, Lupton, AZ 86508
(928) 688-2448

Tomahawk Indian Store
Interstate 40, Exit 359, Lupton, AZ 86508
(928) 688-2596

Chee's Indian Store
Allentown Road N, Houck, AZ 86506
(928) 688-2433, www.cheesindianstore.com

Indian City Arts & Crafts
PO Box 137, Houck, AZ 86506
(928) 688-2691

Fort Courage Trading Post
N. Frontage Road, Houck, AZ 86506
(928) 688-2233

Indian Ruins Trading Post
Interstate 40, Exit 341, Sanders, AZ 86512
(928) 688-2787

Route 66 Diner
Arizona Park Estates, Sanders, AZ 86512
(928) 688-3537

Hubbell Trading Post National Historic Site
PO Box 150, Ganado, AZ
(928) 755-3475, www.nps.gov/hutr

Petrified Forest & Painted Desert

Petrified Forest National Park
PO Box 2217, Petrified Forest, AZ 86028
(928) 524-3567, www.nps.gov/pefo

Stewart's Petrified Wood Shop
PO Box 68, Holbrook, AZ 86025
(800) 4114-8533, www.petrifiedwood.com

Painted Desert Indian Center
9345 Highway 66, Holbrook, AZ 86025
(928) 524-2277

Holbrook

Navajo County Courthouse and Holbrook Visitor Center
100 East Carter, Holbrook, AZ 86025
(928) 524-4223, www.holbrookchamber.com

Joe & Aggie's Café
120 West Hopi Drive, Holbrook AZ 86025
(928) 524-6540, www.joeandaggiescafe.com

Wigwam Motel
811 West Hopi Drive, Holbrook, AZ 86025
(928) 524-3048, www.sleepinawigwam.com

Geronimo Indian Store
Interstate 40, Exit 280, Holbrook, AZ 86025
(928) 288-3241

Rainbow Rock Shop
101 Navajo Boulevard, Holbrook, AZ 86025
(928) 524-2384

Jackrabbit Trading Post
3386 West Highway 66, Joseph City, AZ 86032
(928) 288-3230, www.jackrabbit-tradingpost.com

Winslow

La Posada
303 East 2nd Street, Winslow, AZ 86047
(928) 289-4366, www.laposada.org

Old Trails Museum
212 North Kinsley Avenue, Winslow, AZ 86047
(928) 289-5861, www.oldtrailsmuseum.org

Winslow Visitor Center
523 West Second Street, Winslow, AZ 86047
(928) 289-2434, winslowarizona.org

Homolovi State Park
Hwy 87, Winslow, AZ 86047
(928) 298-4106, azstateparks.com/parks/HORU

Meteor Crater
Interstate 40, Exit 233, Winslow, AZ 86047
(928) 289-5898, www.meteorcrater.com

Meteor City Trading Post
Interstate 40, Exit 239, Meteor City, AZ

Twin Arrows Trading Post
I-40, Exit 219, Twin Arrows, AZ
www.twinarrowsaz.com

Flagstaff

Flagstaff Visitor Center
One East Route 66, Flagstaff, AZ 86001
(800) 842-7293, www.flagstaffarizona.org

Walnut Canyon National Monument
Walnut Canyon Road, Flagstaff, AZ 86004
(928) 526-3367, www.nps.gov/waca

Sunset Crater Volcano National Monument
Forest Service Road 545, Flagstaff, AZ 86004
(928) 526-0502, www.nps.gov/sucr

Wupatki National Monument
Forest Service Road 545, Flagstaff, AZ 86004
(928) 679-2365, www.nps.gov/wupa

The Museum Club
3404 East Route 66, Flagstaff, AZ 86004
(928) 526-9434, www.themuseumclub.com

Miz Zip's
2924 East Route 66, Flagstaff, AZ 86004
(928) 526-0104

Route 66 Dog Haus
1302 East Route 66, Flagstaff, AZ 86001
(928) 774-3211

Hotel Weatherford
23 North Leroux Street, Flagstaff, AZ 86001
(928) 779-1919, www.weatherfordhotel.com

Hotel Monte Vista
100 North San Francisco Street,
Flagstaff, AZ 86001
(928) 779-6971, www.hotelmontevista.com

Lowell Observatory
1400 West Mars Hill Road,
Flagstaff, AZ 86001
(928) 774-3358, www.lowell.edu

Galaxy Diner
931 West Route 66, Flagstaff, AZ 86001
(928) 774-2466

Arboretum of Flagstaff
4001 South Woody Mountain Road,
Flagstaff, AZ 86001
(928) 774-1442, www.thearb.org

Route 66 Roadhouse Bar & Grill
11840 West Route 66, Bellemont, AZ 86015
(928) 774-5080

Slide Rock State Park
6871 North Highway 89A, Sedona, AZ 86336
(928) 282-3034, azstateparks.com/parks/SLRO

Williams

Parks Feed and Mercantile
518 North Parks Road, Parks, AZ 86018
(928) 635-1310

Grand Canyon Deer Farm
6769 East Deer Farm Road,
Williams, AZ 86046
(928) 635-4073, www.deerfarm.com

Williams Visitor Center
200 West Railroad Avenue, Williams, AZ 86046
(800) 863-0546, www.experiencewilliams.com

Grand Canyon Railway
235 North Grand Canyon Boulevard, Williams,
AZ 86046
(928) 773-1976, www.thetrain.com

Bearizona
1500 East Route 66, Williams, AZ 86046
(928) 635-2289, www.bearizona.com

Cruiser's Café 66
233 West Route 66, Williams, AZ 86046
(928) 635-2445, www.cruisers66.com

Pete's Route 66 Gas Station Museum
101 East Route 66, Williams, AZ 86046
(928) 635-2675

Rod's Steak House
301 E. Route 66, Williams, AZ 86046
(928) 635-2671, www.rods-steakhouse.com

Twisters 50's Soda Fountain
417 East Route 66, Williams, AZ 86046
(928) 635-0266, www.route66place.com

Goldie's Route 66 Diner
425 East Route 66, Williams, AZ 86046
(928) 635-4466, www.goldiesroute66diner.com

Pine Country Restaurant
107 North Grand Canyon Boulevard, Williams,
AZ 86046
(928) 635-9718, pinecountryrestaurant.com

The Lodge on Route 66
200 East Route 66, Williams, AZ 86046
(928) 635-4534, thelodgeonroute66.com

Red Garter Bed and Bakery
137 West Railroad Avenue, Williams, AZ
86046
(800) 328-1484, redgarter.com

Grand Canyon Hotel
145 West Route 66, Williams, AZ 86046
(928) 635-1419, thegrandcanyonhotel.com

Planes of Fame Air Museum/Valle Airport
555 South State Road 64, Williams, AZ 86046
(928) 635-1000, www.valleairport.com,
www.planesoffame.org

Grand Canyon National Park
PO Box 129, Grand Canyon, AZ 86023
(928) 638-7888, www.nps.gov/grca

Ash Fork Route 66 Museum
901 West Route 66, Ash Fork, AZ 86320
(928) 637-0204, ashforkrt66museum.com

Seligman

**Delgadillo's Route 66 Gift Shop
& Visitor Center**
22265 West Route 66, Seligman, AZ 86337
(928) 422-3352, www.route66giftshop.com

Twisters 50's Soda Fountain in Williams.

Black Cat Bar
22380 West Route 66, Seligman, AZ 86337
(928) 422-3451, blackcatbar-seligman.com

Delgadillo's Snow Cap Drive-In
22235 East Route 66, Seligman, AZ 86337
(928) 422-3291

Historic Seligman Sundries
22405 Route 66, Seligman, AZ 86337
(928) 853-0051, www.seligmansundries.com

Supai Motel
22450 Route 66, Seligman, AZ 86337
(928) 422-4153, www.supaimotel.com

Historic Route 66 Motel
22750 West Route 66, Seligman, AZ 86337
(928) 422-3204

Westside Lilo's Café
22855 West Route 66, Seligman, AZ 86337
(928) 442-5456, www.westsideliloscafe.com

Peach Springs to Hackberry

Grand Canyon Caverns
Route 66, Mile Post Marker 115
(928) 422-3223, www.gccaverns.com

Hualapai Lodge
889 Highway Street, Peach Springs, AZ 86434
(928) 769-2230, hualapaitourism.com

The Frontier Café
16118 Route 66, Peach Springs, AZ 86434
(928) 769-2237

Keepers of the Wild Nature Park
13441 East Route 66, Valentine, AZ 86437
(928) 769-1800, www.keepersofthewild.org

Hackberry General Store
11255 East Route 66, Hackberry, AZ 86411
(928) 769-2605, hackberrygeneralstore.com

Kingman

Kingman Army Airfield Museum
4540 Flightline Drive, Kingman, AZ 86401
(928) 757-1892, www.main.
kingmanaafhsmuseum.org

Historic Route 66 Association of Arizona
120 West Route 66, Kingman, AZ 86401
(928) 753-5001, www.azrt66.com

Kingman Powerhouse Visitors Center
120 West Route 66, Kingman, AZ 86401
(928) 753-6106

Mohave Museum of History and Arts
400 West Beale Street, Kingman, AZ 86401
(928) 753-3195, www.mohavemuseum.org

Mr. D'z Route 66 Diner
105 East Andy Devine Avenue,
Kingman, AZ 86401
(928) 718-0066, www.mrdzrt66diner.com

Hill Top Motel
1901 East Andy Devine Avenue, Kingman, AZ
86401, (928) 753-2198, www.hilltopmotelaz.com

Redneck's Southern Pit BBQ
420 East Beale Street, Kingman, AZ 86401
(928) 757-8227,
www.redneckssouthernpitbbq.com

Cool Springs Camp
8275 West Oatman Road, Kingman, AZ 86413
(928) 768-8366, www.coolspringsroute66.com

Oatman and Lake Havasu

Oatman Hotel
181 Oatman-Topock Highway, Oatman, AZ
86433, (928) 768-4408

Havasu National Wildlife Refuge
(760) 326-3853, www.fws.gov/southwest/
refuges/Arizona/havasu

London Bridge/Lake Havasu
Lake Havasu City Convention
& Visitors Bureau
314 London Bridge Road,
Lake Havasu City, AZ 86403
(928) 453-3444, www.golakehavasu.com

Acknowledgments

The author wishes to acknowledge the invaluable assistance of several people. Sean Evans, who generously shared his historical expertise, Cline Library for their resources, Route 66 Association of Arizona for doing the heavy lifting, Mike Ward for his lavish collection of vintage postcards, Heather Herman for getting the social media ball rolling, Laura Pruitt for her work on the website and especially Angel Delgadillo for being the most visionary small-town barber in history. Thanks to the Rio Nuevo folks: Ross Humphreys and David Jenney for the opportunity, Caroline Cook for her graceful editing, and Julie Sullivan for her swinging design. And a heartfelt thanks to Tom Griswold for making a move to Arizona possible, Jill Cassidy for taking a chance on an unproven writer and Martin Kuz for his relentless support and cherished friendship.

The photography in this book was inspired by four special people. My dad, George, a B-17 gunner who trained at Kingman Army Airfield, returned from the war to build landmark neon signs and show me the ropes. My mother, Shirley, curious about the world, a writer of many published stories, has shown me the wonders of travel. My brother, Scott, an athlete who believes in me constantly. And my wife, Wendy, a soulful teacher, dancer, artist, gardener, gourmet cook, and loving travel companion.

The Author and Photographer

Roger Naylor is a freelance writer, and his work appears regularly in Arizona Highways, Arizona Republic, Las Vegas Review-Journal, Sedona Magazine, and Nevada Magazine. He is a senior writer for The Bob and Tom Show, a nationally syndicated radio program. Roger lives in Cottonwood, Arizona.

Larry Lindahl's photography has been showcased in books, scenic calendars, and magazines, including Arizona Highways, Outdoor Photographer, Smart Money, American Archaeology, and Southwest Art. He is author and photographer of the award-winning book, Secret Sedona: Sacred Moments in the Landscape. Larry lives in Sedona, Arizona.

www.facebook.com/Route66Arizona